Praise for Practically Shameless

"In this priceless book, Alyce Barry reveals with the freshness and innocence of a child's eyes what her heart is truly filled with—love!! A real gem."
—**Leland Howe**, author, coach and consultant

"Alyce's humor, pain and humanity shine through in this intimate memoir. Reading her generous account of life 'in the box' and eventual redemption moved me to tears, laughter and a deep peace."
—**Joe Laur**, Shadow Work facilitator and coach

"Alyce takes us on her amazing journey as she reclaims her joy and her soul. So many heart-touching insights to show us that we can heal, and exactly how."
—**Bill Kauth**, author of *A Circle of Men* and co-founder of the ManKind Project

"Written with simplicity and incredible depth, Alyce takes the very complex concepts of Shadow Work and creates a doorway for both the beginner and those experienced in Shadow Work. If you want to take the risk to deepen your life, read this book. Your life will be transformed."
—**Char Tosi**, Founder, Woman Within Training

"*Practically Shameless* is a page-turner detective story. Alyce Barry is a sleuth stalking her most feared foes until these villains are hers. Her trail teaches us ways to welcome any part of our being with non-violence and compassion."
—**Jude Blitz**, M.A., Hakomi therapist and Shadow Work facilitator

"Alyce Barry allows us to see her shadow and in the process we see more clearly our own. I highly recommend this book to anyone who is tired of living in a box."
—**John Lee**, author of *The Flying Boy* and *The Missing Peace*

"Completely amazing. A very healing book that could lead to a wonderful discovery of self."
—**David Hicks**, Ph.D., author of *Writing Through Literature*

"I couldn't put it down; I was cheering on this courageous woman as she fought for her life and won."
—**Lyman Coleman**, author of *Serendipity Bible for Groups* and other books

"Alyce's personal journey through Shadow Work will inspire and encourage newcomers to self-development. A book for those you really care about—including yourself."
—**Father Thomas Miller**, Pastor and Shadow Work coach

"*Practically Shameless* is a delightfully easy read that created a container for my own deepest thoughts. I recommend this book to anyone starting their own journey."
—**Ginny Drewes**, Shadow Work facilitator and coach

Practically Shameless

How Shadow Work
Helped Me Find
My Voice, My Path,
and My Inner Gold

Alyce Barry

With a foreword by Cliff Barry
Illustrations by Cindy Kalman

Practically Shameless Press
Longmont, Colorado, USA

Shadow Work is a registered trademark of Shadow Work Seminars, Inc., Boulder, Colorado

Grateful acknowledgment is made to Shambhala Publications for permission to reprint a quatrain from *Unseen Rain: Quatrains of Rumi* by Coleman Barks. Copyright © 1986 by Coleman Barks.

Grateful acknowledgment is made to Random House, Inc., for permission to reprint a portion of *Memories, Dreams, Reflections* by C. G. Jung. Recorded and edited by Aniela Jaffé. Translated from the German by Richard and Clara Winston. The portion appears on page 292 of the April 1989 Vintage Books paperback edition.

Cover and interior design by Nick Zelinger, www.nzgraphics.com
Illustrations by Cindy Kalman, www.kalmarx.com
Photo of the author by Michelle Maloy Dillon, www.mmdphotography.com

Publisher's Cataloging-in-Publication
(Provided by Quality Books, Inc.)

Barry, Alyce.
    Practically shameless : how shadow work helped me
find my voice, my path, and my inner gold / by Alyce
Barry ; foreword by Cliff Barry ; illustrations by Cindy
Kalman.
    p. cm.
    Includes index.
    LCCN 2007933486
    ISBN-13: 978-0-9798326-1-1
    ISBN-10: 0-9798326-1-6

1. Self-actualization (Psychology) 2. Shame.
I. Title.

BF637.S4B37 2008   158.1
                        QBI07-600205

PO Box 1505, Longmont, Colorado 80502-1505, USA
www.PracticallyShameless.com

Printed in the United States of America

DISCLAIMER

The descriptions in this book of Shadow Work processes are not intended as a substitute for psychological counseling or medical advice, or for Shadow Work done with a certified Shadow Work professional.

Neither are these descriptions intended as training in Shadow Work facilitation, and the steps and techniques involved in and essential to the successful implementation of certain of these processes have been intentionally abridged, omitted and/or obscured. The reader should not attempt to facilitate himself/herself or any other person or persons through any process mentioned in this book without first obtaining the appropriate Shadow Work training. The author and publisher disclaim any responsibility or liability resulting from ignoring this caution. Training in Shadow Work facilitation is available only from certified Shadow Work trainers. For more information on available trainings, visit www.ShadowWork.com/Trainings.

The exercise in Chapter 19 should not be performed while driving, operating equipment, or otherwise engaged in activity that could prove hazardous when done conjointly with experiencing the exercise. The author and publisher disclaim any responsibility or liability resulting from ignoring this caution.

To my father, John Edward Barry, 1924 – 1990

Dad holding Cliff, 1949

"I have lived on the lip

of insanity, wanting to know reasons,

knocking on a door. It opens.

I've been knocking from the inside!"

~ Rumi

Contents

Foreword

If there's anything I can't stand, it's another ten-step process that promises to fix all my troubles in an instant. I have been promised too much too often. I don't believe the promises any more. And yet, as someone who creates and sells personal growth processes, I must always compete with the other offerings in the marketplace. I sometimes see myself as the quiet chick in the nest, unwilling to squawk for food alongside my siblings because I'm tired of making all that noise.

So I don't get the big worm.

Since creating Shadow Work, I have wanted it to be well seasoned. I have wanted it to be tested. I did not want to make claims that were spurious or superficial. And most of all, I have wanted the *way* I promoted Shadow Work to be in line with the deep principles of the work itself. So Shadow Work has grown slowly. And it has matured well, if I do say so myself.

Shadow Work facilitators don't take short cuts. They will not sell you something in a way that betrays you or tricks you. They will not belittle you just because they can't see a way to motivate you naturally. They will not confront you unnecessarily just so *they* don't feel small. So I'm happy with the way we have grown so far.

And now there is this wonderful book, written by my sister, which can take you right inside the processes that Shadow Work offers. Alyce has offered to be your guide and show you what her journey was like and how you might benefit from some of what she discovered.

I am immensely proud of what Alyce has done here. She has also avoided the short cuts. No squawking. Instead, she devoted her life to the process of writing this book. She followed that process, wherever it led her, for almost seven years. It led her through her own dark places, where she really had to practice what she preaches here.

Her dedication has been an inspiration to me. I thought I was the only one in the family crazy enough to devote myself that completely to a dream. But now I have her company. We are both nuts for this work. And we both believe that it's possible to create real change in your life without shaming yourself along the way. We think you can grow in a way that honors your natural growth cycle, that does not require you to supercharge yourself into a frenzy as if you were a runner vaulting over hurdles in a race.

Sometimes, if you study a hurdle carefully, you can find a way to transcend it that doesn't require you to maintain a frenzied state of momentum. Frenzy gets tiring. Nobody can keep it up indefinitely. You may sprint ahead, but then you get winded and often backslide.

Shadow Work offers you a different way to approach the hurdle. It offers you a more natural way to grow that can integrate into your existing lifestyle more easily, without the self-contorting effort it takes to meet hurdle after hurdle after hurdle.

Let me give you an example.

If you are like most people, you sometimes tell yourself that you live "in your head" too much. (If this example isn't true for you, you may know someone for whom it does fit). In personal growth workshops especially, or in therapy, you may have been coached to "get out of your head and into your feelings!" Maybe you have been "confronted" by the therapist or facilitator as a way to force you into your anger. Or maybe you have been "challenged" to "bust through" into your real joy.

I'm not saying that busting through doesn't work. It does. At first. And real progress is made. But eventually you get tired of "busting through" all the time. Or, worse, you become one of those people who never lets anyone else rest, who "busts" everybody around them all the time with your surefire, ten-step process.

In Shadow Work, we take a little extra time to really study the hurdle you want to jump. We look, in particular, to see if the way you are defining the problem is shaming you in some way. Shaming yourself creates solutions that are harder than they need to be. So, for example, if you think you need to get into your feelings more, we might direct our attention to your belief that you are "in your head." We might suggest that you aren't actually in your head and out of touch with your emotions at all. We might suggest that when you are in the state you call being "in your head," you are actually scared of something. You are afraid.

Here's the news flash: *fear is an emotion!* When you are in the state you call being "in your head," you are actually in touch with one of your emotions: the emotion of fear. Telling yourself that you are out of touch with your emotions is mostly a shaming story you may have learned to tell about yourself. The story represents you as uncaring or unloving. It tells you that you are a cold fish with a small or shriveled heart. That's nonsense. It's not possible for a human being to stop feeling. You may feel ashamed. You may feel afraid. But you are feeling all of the time. You can't stop.

So, if you want to be more in touch with your emotions, you can begin by recognizing the emotion you are already experiencing rather than telling yourself that you are not having any emotions at all. It's an approach that *lifts some shame off you*, and when you feel less shame, you are more likely to connect with your feelings. It often stimulates a sense of a fresh start, which can be very motivating in itself. And it's easier, too. It's easier to do more of something you are already doing than it is to figure out how to start doing something that you think you are not doing at all.

If you often tell yourself you are "in your head" too much, it might help you to realize how often you actually feel afraid. For many people the feeling of fear is like the water in the aquarium that the fish swims in: it's invisible to the fish. The fish only sees what is beyond the water that completely surrounds its body.

You probably learned to tolerate this low-level fear quite early in life because you were constantly in situations where it was *smart* to be afraid. You probably learned to feel this background fear without even noticing that you were afraid.

How many times in your life do you think you've been told "Don't be afraid!" or "There's nothing to fear here!" But if you ask yourself what you are afraid of in this moment, you will find that you can fill a page with your answers. If you are willing to pay attention to the times when you are thinking that you are "in your head" and remember to think that you are actually "feeling afraid," you will no longer need to supercharge yourself into a frenzy that will carry you over the hurdle. The hurdle will simply disappear because it was based on a perspective that is no longer true for you.

But here's the catch: most people don't actually want to know that they are afraid that much of the time. So next you might want to learn *what to do* when you are afraid. You can learn lots about that in this book. You can learn to honor the part of you that has been protecting you all the time you were afraid even if you didn't know you were afraid. And once you have honored that part, it can become your clever ally when you're afraid. You will feel a lot safer even when you move into your other feelings.

That is an example of the Shadow Work approach: to examine the hurdle closely enough that you find out if it is really there and if it is not, to reveal it as the mirage it always was. When hurdles start disappearing, you can start to feel practically shameless—as Alyce and I and many others who facilitate Shadow Work do.

Read on to examine with Alyce many more ways to shift your perspective on yourself away from shame and toward the more natural approach to growth that is represented by Shadow Work.

Cliff Barry
Boulder, Colorado, 2007

Introduction

You can change, even if you have tried, repeatedly, with little success. You can be happier than you are today. You can get more of what you've been wanting from life. I've done it, and you can, too.

This book is about the human shadow. Shadow could be called "the box built by shame." Healing the shame transforms the box into precisely the life you have always wanted.

A lot has been written about the box: inside vs. outside, how to think outside it, how to *get* outside it. The box is our collective metaphor for the shadow, and what an apt metaphor it is. Like a box, the shadow traps us in behaviors that seem impossible to change. We feel like prisoners inside our own minds and hearts.

But this is *not* another book about how to think outside the box— because the answer to the box is not outside but *through*. The box is a delivery room, perfectly designed to birth the life you want. Perfectly designed to help you become practically shameless.

This book is the story of a box I was trapped in for more than forty years. I've used the story to illustrate where a box comes from, how it gets built, what it is made of, what gets trapped inside it, why it is so hard to change, and how it can be transformed.

No matter what kind of box you've been trapped in, you can transform it, from the inside out, just as I did. You can go through the delivery room and birth the new life you want. You can lift the shame off yourself and love yourself unconditionally. You can make conscious choices instead of reacting to your buttons getting pushed. You can bring your authentic self out of shadow and act from it, rather than trying to be who you think you *should* be.

You can start changing now, as you unlock the secrets of the box.

Chapter 1

Inside My Box

We never stop wanting what we want, even when it looks as if we'll never get it.

When I was nine years old, what I wanted was to belong in a group of girls my age. I was the third of five children and I was lonely at home, marooned between two older siblings who were close in age and two younger brothers who were playmates. I wanted to nestle into a group of girls the way a puppy nestles into the pile. I wanted to be one of the girls.

But I had a problem: I sometimes said mean things to the other girls. I didn't intend to be mean, but it happened anyway—I opened my mouth and mean things came out. A girl in my class had a speech impediment and I made fun of the way she talked. When someone made a mistake, I was the first to point it out and the first to laugh. I remember telling one friend, who had knitted herself a sweater and worn it proudly to school every day ever since, that her sweater was the color of mud.

Of course, my remarks got a reaction from the other girls. "You're so mean," they said. I didn't want to believe it, because it hurt. Mean people were bad. The other girls were saying I was bad. *I* couldn't really be bad, not *me*. Could I?

Maybe, I thought, *I'm just being clever and they don't understand.* When I tried to explain what was so funny, they said, "No, you're just being mean."

Finally, I could no longer deny it. There were many of them and only one of me; they must be right. I must be mean, and that meant I was bad. I wanted them to like me, and they wouldn't if I was bad. So I had to hide my badness away where they wouldn't see it.

I had to hide that I was bad. My badness only became evident when I talked. The answer was to stop talking. I don't think it was a conscious decision. I couldn't think about it very clearly because it hurt so much.

TESTING THE THEORY

I learned to sit quietly and listen while the other girls talked. At least I'm still with them, I told myself. I'm still one of the girls.

But inside me there was anger. The other girls could talk, why couldn't I? As I listened to them, I thought of clever things to say. When I kept those clever things to myself, I felt angry and frustrated. My frustration built up until I thought I would burst.

Talking couldn't be worse than this, I thought to myself, and I went ahead and spoke. Sometimes it came out okay, and I felt a huge relief. Then I opened up and said more. But eventually something mean came out of my mouth. Then the other girls told me, "You're so mean."

Somehow my badness was slipping out anyway. Maybe I just needed to try harder. When I thought of saying something, I quickly stuffed it down. The harder I stuffed myself, though, the angrier I got. The angrier I got, the more likely I was to blurt out something mean.

Time spent with other girls became charged with frustration and anxiety. I told myself I was worrying about it too much. I just needed to think about something else. I decided to focus on the games we played. But for some reason, that didn't work for long either. The more I focused on the game, the angrier I got if I didn't win, and the more likely I was to make a mean remark to the girl who had won.

There seemed to be no way to win, no way to fit in and be one of the girls. In bed at night, I cried, hugging the loneliness to me. There was something sweet about the pain in my heart, as if I were hugging to me a stuffed animal with real claws.

When I couldn't take the pain any more, I clutched at a cover story: I didn't fit in because I was a tomboy. I enjoyed climbing trees and playing baseball with the boys. Girls weren't as fun to play with anyway. Somewhere beneath my cover story, though, I knew I was bad, and it hurt.

THE EDITOR APPEARS

In high school the pattern repeated with a new set of girls. I told one girl she was cheap for making out with her boyfriend. I told another that if she couldn't quit smoking it meant she was just lazy. I told a girl in art class she had about as much artistic talent as mud. (I seemed to have a thing about mud.) The other girls called me "critical," the high school word for mean.

I tried the same tactics as before: sitting silently, focusing on something else. Nothing worked. I withdrew into time alone. I almost wore out the sad songs on my records by playing them over and over. I became a photographer for the school yearbook and tried relating to people from the other end of a lens. My favorite tactic was surprise: I walked up behind a classmate and got a candid, informal shot when she turned around. It was easier than trying to create a comfortable connection with her.

One thing, however, had changed since elementary school: I had begun to edit myself inside my head. When I thought of something to say, I analyzed it carefully first. Was it critical? If it wasn't, was it irrelevant or unnecessary? In other words, was there anything questionable about it? I had to know because if there was, I would get sliced and diced for it afterward from the voice in my head that I had come to think of as my Editor.

Of course, once a comment passed all the tests, the right moment had often passed by the time I spoke it aloud. Then my Editor told me how foolish I had sounded. Even if I was still on topic, and even if my comment had sounded witty inside my head, it now sounded clumsy and stupid. Or so my Editor convinced me.

Before, I had felt bad when I said something critical. Now I felt bad even before I opened my mouth. My Editor was never happy with anything I wanted to say or with how I finally said it. I felt bad nearly all the time, about nearly all the thoughts in my head, whether I was saying them or not.

I even edited myself when I was alone. I had begun writing poetry, and my favorite thing about it was the first burst of inspiration, when the words burned like fever and sang like music. As soon as I finished a first draft, though, the Editor began to tear it apart.

"No, no," it said, "this is all wrong." It said I had a poor vocabulary, that my writing was boring, clumsy, stupid, obvious, clichéd.

I crossed out my original words and tried new ones. For a brief moment, the new words gleamed with originality and freshness— they were *alive*! Then the Editor got at them, and I crossed them out again. Sometimes I edited and revised and rewrote a poem so many times that it became unrecognizable. The paper ran with red ink like blood. Slowly, painfully, the poem died. There was nothing left to do but throw it away and wait for the next inspiration to strike.

Before long, the Editor insisted on having a hand before I had even finished a first draft. "This is terrible," it said. "You'll have to start over from the beginning. And do it right this time!"

I returned to the first few lines, trying desperately to get them just right. I edited and re-edited instead of moving forward. The earlier in a poem I began editing, the less likely I was to finish it.

After a while, it was painful just getting an inspiration. I knew I would suffer agonies and only rarely have the satisfaction of finishing. I began resisting the urge to write down the words that came. At first, not writing them down felt like smothering a baby with a pillow, but it gradually got easier. Better a quick death than a slow agony, went my cover story. Somewhere deep inside, though, I was afraid something was wrong with me, and it hurt.

A NEW LABEL

After high school, I went to work in the office world and made a living typing what other people wrote. A boyfriend who had majored in mathematics told me, "If either of us is a writer, it's me, not you!" A part of me wanted to believe him; it would mean no more babies to smother. Another part of me was grief-stricken, but I shut myself off to its grief.

I befriended coworkers but had few interpersonal skills, and none of these friendships lasted long. I heard someone use the word "loner" to mean someone who enjoyed being alone more than with others. I decided that must be what I was. I certainly spent a lot of time alone, listening to sad music and watching movies. I took a certain comfort from having a word that explained it. At least I had a diagnosis for what was wrong with me. At night, I hugged it to me, feeling that same sweet pain.

THE VALUE OF FRIENDSHIP

When I married my mathematician boyfriend, I thought that he would be my all-in-all and I would never be lonely again. We moved to an area where we knew no one, and I made no effort to find friends.

When the marriage ended badly, though, I realized I had been wrong. He'd had a breakdown once before, and as he descended into madness, there was no one who knew us who could give me a reality check. No one I could confide in. I realized that friendships outside a marriage were crucial to its survival. I vowed to do things differently next time.

In the meantime, my urge to write had resurfaced, partly as therapy to help me work through what had happened. Now I wanted to write not poetry but biographies of America's founding fathers. I returned to college to get a degree in history and began to think of myself as an intellectual. I loved my hours of research in the library, though I was trying without success to connect with people who had been dead for nearly two hundred years. As a college student in my late twenties, I didn't make many friends among my much younger classmates. When I felt lonely, I consoled myself with the belief that I would contribute scholarship of importance.

I began research for a biography of Thomas Paine, a man with a biting tongue of his own and few friends, who had died penniless and alone. I felt sure he had been misunderstood and under-appreciated by his contemporaries, even those he had attacked viciously in his writings. When I fell in love again, the man who would become my second husband remarked that a biography of Paine was hardly relevant to our modern times.

A veil seemed to fall from my eyes. What had I been thinking? I couldn't write well enough to do this! Writing the definitive biography would require lengthy research in France, and I loved being in love again. When I stopped writing, that was my cover story: I gave it up for love. Somewhere beneath my cover story, though, I was grief-stricken. Other people wrote books, why couldn't I? There must be something wrong with me, and it hurt.

After college, I went to work for a publishing company and helped other people get published.

When we married, I remembered what I had learned from my first marriage and reached out to the wives of my husband's friends. Here I encountered an unexpected obstacle: these women talked about clothes, shopping, makeup, entertaining. I had never known much about these topics and had spent my free time for several years being the scholar, where such things were of little importance. I criticized these women inside my head for being shallow, focused on appearances, not interested as I was in the life of the mind. And of course, I felt guilty and ashamed for what I was thinking. The same old pattern had emerged.

I withdrew again. My cover story, in which I played the intellectual who was above such artificial pursuits, was as thin as paper. I wanted so much to have friends. What was wrong with me?

THINKING OUTSIDE THE BOX

Shortly after my daughter was born, I read an article in a women's magazine about the value for a young mother to have close female friends. A longing arose inside me. How wonderful it would be to share my experiences of motherhood with another woman. I suddenly had a new thought: *Maybe making friends wasn't really that hard after all! Everyone does this, I've just been thinking about it all wrong!* It was as if a fresh breeze were blowing through the house. I was thinking outside the box.

I started a mom-and-tot play group of women from my neighborhood. I called the first meeting and bounded into it like an overeager puppy. This time it will work, I told myself. This time it will be easy! I'll just be different!

And for a while, I was. My puppy strategy was to be upbeat, positive, and never say anything negative or critical. I leapt from topic to topic to keep the conversation on a lighthearted note. I uttered any thought that entered my head, even if it was silly, artificial or phony. Something inside me shuddered to hear such counterfeit comments coming out of my mouth. I tried hard not to listen. I had friends! A new future beckoned and I believed I was finally free of the past.

It wasn't long, however, before I found myself having what seemed like very judgmental thoughts about the other women and their children. This woman here seemed awfully controlling toward her child. That baby was really pretty ugly. Maybe these women wanted to get together only so they could whine about their husbands.

Being the puppy was not the solution I had hoped for. I was trying so hard to be lighthearted that any real connection with the other women was out of the question. My new friends were acquaintances, no more. I would no more have reached out to them for support than I would to strangers walking down the sidewalk.

My spirits slowly sank. I had long since forgotten the pleasure of that fresh breeze. All I knew was that I was once again feeling guilty and ashamed in a group of women. It didn't matter what I said aloud because my Editor was slicing and dicing me for what I was thinking. I went quiet and eventually stopped attending, and the group disbanded. This time my sadness became depression, though I didn't admit that to myself until years later.

I hungered for a circle of friends and longed to express myself creatively. But I couldn't connect with other women or my own creativity because there was a wall in my way. The wall was my Editor, telling me I was too critical for a group and too lacking in talent to write. I kept hurling myself at the wall, hoping I could change and failing every time. I was trapped and lonely and unable to change.

Chapter 2

Calls for Help

O n a Saturday afternoon in the summer of 1995 my life began to change. It started when my phone rang.

I was forty-four years old, living in a suburb of Chicago with my husband and ten-year-old daughter. For eight years I had been working as a technical writer, writing software manuals for mainframe computers. After years in secretarial jobs, this was my first salaried job with the word "Writer" in the title. I had learned technical writing while in an administrative job, and getting paid to write still seemed too good to be true. In fact, the first time I wrote "Writer" in the occupation box on my income tax form, my eyes filled with tears. Technical writing wasn't creative, or so I told myself, but it was writing.

I had one woman friend, Libby Brewer, whom I had known since second grade. She and I had recently reconnected. Because she was a year younger, I didn't associate her with my painful group experiences with girls in my own class. We saw each other every six weeks or so and I finally had a woman friend I could really talk to. It would be overstating it, though, to say we were close. There were huge areas of our lives (sex, for example) that we never discussed.

LIFE IN THE BOX

In 1995, if you had asked me what I thought of myself, I would have said, "I'm good at technical writing." If I had been self-aware enough to express what I really thought, I would have added, "I can't be trusted to do anything right."

I worked hard and drew what little self-worth I had from what I got done. I could look at a shelf of manuals I had written at the office. But it often seemed work was all there was. Life was a treadmill of doing. I had no idea how to have fun. My husband and I occasionally talked to a marriage counselor about how to have fun together, and about how to fight with each other, but we never learned to do either.

I believed myself to be an ethical person, but there was no god in my world. I had been raised in a religious community and had turned my back on God when my first marriage ended so disastrously. I had decided that God and religion had betrayed me. But I was terrified of death and had nightmares about horrible things happening to me and my loved ones.

I enjoyed spending money. I enjoyed eating, especially anything containing chocolate. For three years in the early 1990s, I had worked a second job, publishing a subscription newsletter on filmmaking in Chicago. I had hoped it would eventually pay well enough to be my only job. It was thrilling to see my writing published, even if for a small audience, and I enjoyed being my own boss. But the cost was working late into the night, and I frequently used brownies as fuel to keep me awake. I ate only brownies topped with chocolate icing—I didn't like those pale brown things the color of mud. (Again with the mud.) It gradually became clear that the newsletter would only lose money, not make it. I gave it up and watched movies on tape instead, tinkering with the dialogue inside my head.

I loved reading novels, but almost never allowed myself to do so because lying on the sofa reading seemed so lazy. I did allow myself the occasional nonfiction book because it taught me something interesting enough to mention in a social conversation. I considered most of my life too boring to talk about.

I didn't take good care of my body and spent a lot of money on chiropractors. I told myself I had a bad back. Every few months my back muscles would rebel against my all-sitting-all-the-time regimen and go into spasm. Then I would lie on the sofa for a few days, adjusting ice packs and watching television. I didn't take good care of my teeth either and spent a lot on dentists, too.

At work, I took whatever salary raises the company offered me and didn't dare ask for more. I was convinced that if my boss really thought about my value to the company, he would figure out I was a waste of money and fire me.

Spending time with my daughter usually involved watching a movie together. I didn't even sit with her. I sat on the sofa while she curled up in her favorite armchair nearby. A movie was the surest way to avoid a request from her to play, a request that invariably terrified me. I was afraid I would not know how or would do the wrong thing. As I sank into the sofa cushions, my body felt leaden.

Once, acting on impulse while she was taking a bath, I concocted a game. I curled my left hand to look like a critter with a mouth that opened wide when I stretched my hand. The critter warbled the song "Singing in the Rain" in a falsetto voice. With my other hand, I poured water over its head from a plastic watering can. When the water ran out, the critter stopped singing and jerked its head from side to side, asking plaintively where the rain had gone.

My daughter squealed with delight and asked me to do it again. Suddenly I was terrified. What if I did it wrong or ran out of things for the critter to say? I managed to repeat the act a few more times, but I had frozen inside. I made some excuse and left the room, feeling utterly pathetic.

I thought of my husband as my best friend, but we rarely showed each other our deepest feelings. Even when I felt depressed, I rarely reached out to him or anyone else for emotional support. I believed I should be self-sufficient. The real reason I didn't ask for support was that I believed I didn't deserve it. I starved myself of most kinds of companionship until I became completely desperate. Then I finally allowed myself to reach out. But it takes effort to build a support network, an effort in which I had never invested, so there was no one there to reach. In that state of desperation, I had no time to wait; I needed help that very instant. If no one was available, I figured I was meant to go it alone and withdrew my outstretched hand. And the cycle began again.

TOO GOOD TO BE TRUE

Besides a creative life, there was something else I wanted, though I hardly dared admit it to myself. I wanted to help people. During my first year of college, I had planned to become a clinical psychologist. I'd had my first look at psychosis with my first husband's breakdown, and it had scared the hell out of me. I wanted to get as far away from it as I could. But the desire to help didn't go away.

In my job as a technical writer, I worked with a computer programmer who was taking night classes to get a degree in computer science. He had to take an English class to fulfill a requirement, and at

34

work one day, he asked me to look over an English paper he had written. I was thrilled that he had asked me but worried that I would do something wrong: that I would say the wrong thing, give him more feedback than he wanted, be too critical. Basically, I was afraid my Editor would tear him to pieces.

I nervously read his essay and marked it up. When he returned to pick it up, I gave him minimal feedback while staring at the paper, at my lap, at the wall—anything to avoid looking him in the face. To my surprise, he thanked me profusely and told me how helpful I had been.

When he walked away, I felt relieved, and then jubilant. I had helped somebody! My heart felt bigger inside my chest and my eyes filled with tears. Within moments, my Editor pointed out that my help had not amounted to much. I had marked up a few sentences on a term paper, for a programmer who had no interest in writing. A paper that would never see the light of day.

"Big deal," my Editor said.

But in times of darkness, I clung to the memories of having helped someone. They meant it was okay I was still alive and taking up space in the world. I had an excuse for living.

When even these memories didn't help, I thought about suicide. There were numerous underpasses on my drive home from work. I could drive into an abutment—a quick and presumably painless way to end it all. I told myself I could never do that to my daughter, leave her to grow up motherless. But that was a cover story. I knew deep down that I would never have the courage to go through with it. In my eyes, I was not only worthless, but a coward to boot.

Looking back at myself in the summer of 1995, I see a woman encased in shame. A woman who believed she had no inherent right to exist. A woman desperate to help people but walking on eggshells for fear she would do it wrong. A woman who couldn't connect with those closest to her or with her own body. A woman with few friends and estranged from her own creative force. A woman with no faith in herself or in life, no sense of meaning or purpose, no joy. A woman who ate too much and starved herself emotionally. A woman living in a box.

ON THE PHONE

On that Saturday afternoon when the phone rang, I picked it up and heard the voice of my older brother, Cliff. Cliff lived about three hours away, near Madison, Wisconsin. We saw each other once or twice a year at holiday and birthday gatherings. There had been years when we had lived at opposite ends of the country and hadn't kept in touch by mail, much less by phone. A call was out of the ordinary.

Cliff was calling to ask for my help. His business had a new website, and he was finding it difficult to write a particular page. He wanted a step-by-step description of the work he did so that visitors to his website could decide if they were interested. He was calling to ask if I, as a writer, might be able to give him some pointers or even help him write the page.

A step-by-step description sounded right up my alley as a technical writer.

"Sure," I said in a calm voice, as if this were nothing out of the ordinary. But my internal response was quite different: I was thrilled almost beyond words. If he was consulting me, it meant I was an expert—I might even have talent! If Cliff had told me he needed just one paragraph, I would still have been thrilled.

I was also happy to think I might be able to help Cliff in some way. He had been a surrogate dad to me and our younger siblings growing up. The best memories I had of our family life were mostly of him.

I knew that Cliff's business was something like group therapy, but I knew no more than that. I had nothing against group therapy for other people; I just knew I would never be caught dead doing it myself. "I'm not good with groups" was my standard line. I associated being in groups with feeling guilty, ashamed, and generally bad about myself.

However, I had seen a therapist for several years to sort through the emotional debris from my first marriage. I had read a few self-help books of the *I'm Okay, You're Okay* variety. My husband and I had been to a marriage counselor. I assumed that for the purposes of helping Cliff, I had at least a passing acquaintance with therapy as subject matter.

A DIFFERENT LANGUAGE

I picked up a pad of paper to take some notes and told Cliff to describe his work. He started talking about "the shadow," a term I had not heard before. He said it meant unconscious parts of the self. I had once seen a movie about Freud and knew what unconscious meant.

Cliff said a person could come to one of his workshops and "do their work," but he clearly did not mean their regular job. He said they could do a "process" like the step-by-step procedure he wanted my help describing. In my head, a process was what happened in a factory when glass jars jiggled along on a conveyor belt as they got filled with spaghetti sauce.

"What does a person do during a 'process'?" I asked.

Cliff said they got in touch with "energies" that had not been available to them before. It was risky, he said, and that was why it was so important to do this work in a "safe container."

My brain translated "container" into a corrugated metal box on the deck of a cargo ship. It had no idea what to do with "energies." Maybe something supernatural, like ghosts?

The more questions I asked, the more confused I got. I had no idea what he was talking about. He seemed to be talking in an entirely different language. After a while, I didn't even know what questions to ask. I knew how to translate technical terms into plain English, but this sounded like another planet entirely.

The word "psycho-babble" suddenly came to mind. I had recently heard a friend use that word to describe some weird new therapies. I wondered if this was the kind of thing she had been talking about. At this point, it would have been easy to change my mind about helping Cliff. As a technical writer, I prided myself on crafting precision documents that were free of ambiguity. I could have said that I was uncomfortable writing about something this unfamiliar to me. I could have said, "Sorry, I don't think I can do this."

But I didn't. I told him I would like to help but I just didn't understand. Cliff suggested that I come to one of his weekend workshops so I could see Shadow Work firsthand. One was scheduled for September, just two months away.

"Maybe then you'll get what I'm talking about," he said. "You don't have to participate in any way if you don't want to. You can just sit in the corner and observe."

Accepting his invitation meant being in a group, which I had avoided like the plague for years. Worse, it was some kind of group therapy. I would probably feel pretty stupid, too, since I could understand nothing Cliff said about it. Attending his workshop meant going *way* out of my comfort zone. The logical thing to do was decline.

But I didn't. I accepted, and I have often asked myself why. One reason, I'm sure, was the chance it offered to spend time with an adored older brother I didn't see very often. But there were much less threatening ways to do that. Another reason was the chance it offered to help someone. That, however, was offset by a corresponding risk of failure. I was, after all, a woman who felt like a pathetic failure for not playing with a child in the bathtub.

There was another, more compelling reason.

THE CALL FROM INSIDE

I heard something in Cliff's voice that I had not heard before. He sounded happy, but that was not unusual. Cliff had always been an upbeat, optimistic person. He was always into something new and eager to talk about it.

I heard in Cliff's voice the kind of contentment a person feels when he has been searching for a long time and has finally found what he was looking for. The kind of contentment a person feels when he knows what he wants to do for the rest of his life. The kind of contentment that was wholly lacking in my life.

The contentment I heard in Cliff's voice called to the parts of me that were trapped in a box and wanted out. It called to the part that wanted to help people and felt she didn't deserve to. To the part that wanted to feel good about herself for who she was, not for what she got done. To the part that wanted a reason for living, not just an excuse. To the part that wanted connection and intimacy and physical well-being. To the part that wanted to create, express herself, and be playful without feeling pathetic. To the part that wanted support instead of starvation. To the part that wanted to believe that her life had meaning and to think no more about ending it.

Chapter 3

———— ∞∞∞ ————

The Walls Emerge

I drove to central Wisconsin on a Friday afternoon that September. The workshop was taking place at a camp used by boys' and girls' clubs during the summer. I had brought with me lots of paper and lots of pens. I pictured myself sitting in a corner, silently taking notes. I decided I would say as little as possible and act the role of observer, sort of like a journalist.

Having parked my bags in the bunkhouse, I walked across the parking area to a large, rustic A-frame surrounded by trees. Cliff greeted me at the seminar room door with a hug that lasted a little longer than I knew how to handle. Cliff's partner, Mary Ellen, gave me a hug, too, and her hug also went on a little too long.

As other participants arrived, I felt a bit lonely and went looking for a cup of tea. As I watched Cliff and Mary Ellen greet people from across the room, I noticed that some people coming in got hugs even longer than mine. When Cliff hugged one man in particular—a tall, slender man he obviously considered a good friend—they rocked back and forth for a while, chuckling. It was a new sight for me.

I looked for a place to sit down. Fifteen floor cushions had been arranged around the edges of a large Oriental rug. I placed my tea, paper and pen in front of one of the cushions and went to the restroom. When I got back, a young man with a military haircut had taken my seat and was happily talking with another man several cushions away. I realized he had not noticed my things sitting there, a foot or so in front of his seat.

I felt so angry I hardly knew what to do with myself. I chose a free cushion on the other side of the room, as far from him as I could get. I knew that I could say something to him about it, and probably should, but decided that I would most likely appear petty and immature. My face was flushed and my mouth set in a grim line as I watched the others take their seats.

INTRODUCTIONS

When it was time to start, Cliff told us to think about what we wanted to get out of the workshop while he played a piece of music that lasted about five minutes. He said we would have a chance to share what we wanted in the circle afterward if we wished.

I didn't like feeling angry at all, so I tried to put it away and think about something else. I noticed that many of the others had their eyes closed, so I closed mine as well. As I listened, I realized that the music had been recorded on synthesizers. As a classical music buff, I did not consider synthesized music "real" music, and I silently shook my head with disdain. I opened my eyes and saw that several people were wiping tears from their cheeks. I felt instantly ashamed for judging the music that others had found touching. It was a reminder of how critical I was, as if I needed the reminder.

Cliff began the introductions. Each of us in turn spoke our name. I was third in line to speak, after Cliff and Mary Ellen, and I felt very aware of everyone's eyes on me, as if there were lights and cameras trained on my face. I spoke my name with a forced smile and said I was there mostly to observe. I was too ashamed to say that I had been judging the music.

A woman in the circle, whom I will call Bonnie, said she was there to deal with her "demon." She said she was in a life-and-death struggle with this dark side of her personality, which controlled and tormented her every waking hour. Her voice choked up, and I found my own eyes welling with tears. I realized that there was no other sound in the room. I had never seen a group listen so closely to what someone was saying. It was almost as if the group had sent out invisible arms to hold her, though none of us had moved.

FOUR SELVES

When we had all spoken, Cliff and Mary Ellen talked for a while about the shadow. They repeated the ideas Cliff had tried to explain to me on the phone, about having a safe container in which to look at the shadow and about doing processes to get in touch with shadow energies. I took a few notes but none of it made much sense to me.

They went on to describe four parts of the self, named the Magician, the Sovereign, the Lover, and the Warrior. The four were like the four directions on a map, each headed in the direction of its own priorities and needs. I formed an image of four housemates who took turns answering the door.

If there was a problem in your life, Mary Ellen said, it meant that one of the four parts of you was partly hidden—it was a direction on the map that was closed to you. A problem, Cliff added, did *not* mean you were bad. On the contrary, it meant something hidden was coming into the light where you could get a good look at it and decide what to do about it.

I liked the sound of this—that having a problem didn't mean you were bad.

To give us an experience of each of our four parts, they led us through a series of group exercises and visualizations. For each visualization, they read aloud a story filled with vivid imagery in which we were the title character, while we stood and acted out the story. In the first story, my Magician was a wise, elderly counselor like Merlin, who viewed all the scenes of my life from a great height and saw them with fresh insight. With Merlin's eyes, I saw that it was possible to view my life as something other than a succession of mistakes. I felt alive with possibility and freedom. When the story ended, I came back to an awareness of the seminar room with great reluctance.

In the next visualization, my Sovereign was a compassionate visionary, like King Arthur, who weighed the decisions I had made and found them worthy of blessing instead of censure. In my Sovereign's robes, I stood on the top of a mountain and used the scepter in my outstretched arm to bless my entire kingdom. Then I cradled my infant self in my arms. As I looked into her eyes, I saw there the desire to live *exactly* the life I had lived. I covered my face with my hands and started to cry.

But my Editor would have none of this blessing.

"This is ludicrous," it said. "You've done nothing but make mistakes."

But something else was answering the Editor, something new and unfamiliar coming from inside me.

"Yes!" it said. It meant *yes* to blessing, *yes* to hope, to joy, to life. I didn't know who or what was speaking, but I knew I wanted hear more of that "Yes!"

In the Lover visualization, I had a harder time imagining anyone as beautiful and as sensual as Guinevere inside me, but I did my best. My Editor thought this one was hilarious.

Last came the Warrior visualization. I imagined that I held a shield in one hand and a sword in the other, and I did battle, like Lancelot, with the obstacles that beset my life. Strength from the sword's hilt infused my arm with a power I had never felt before. I *could* change my life, I didn't have to go on this way any longer.

As the group ended for the night, there were a hundred questions I wanted to ask. Asking them felt risky, though. It would mean feeling more lights and cameras on my face, and afterward my Editor slicing and dicing me for any question that sounded stupid. I stayed quiet.

BONNIE'S DEMON

It was on Saturday morning that Cliff and Mary Ellen said they were ready if someone wanted help with an issue. Bonnie got to her feet and stepped out into the middle of the Oriental rug. She wanted to do a "process," as Cliff had tried to describe to me. It meant that she would take a series of steps in order to get something she wanted.

Bonnie said she wanted to shut up her demon so she could get some rest. Cliff suggested that she start by asking someone to play her demon. She asked a man named Wally, who agreed. Cliff asked Bonnie some questions about the demon: Where was it in the room and what was it like? When she placed it in the center of the room, draped it in black, and gave it a line to speak, the demon came to life. Under Bonnie's direction, Wally played the role of the demon by strutting arrogantly to and fro, ranting in a threatening tone and punctuating his words with aggressive gestures.

When Bonnie was satisfied with Wally's portrayal of the demon,

Mary Ellen took her to the far end of the room to observe it from a distance. They watched as Wally strutted and gestured and ranted. Mary Ellen asked Bonnie how she reacted when she saw a demon like this, and Bonnie instinctively turned on her heel, as if to flee in fear. Bonnie chose a woman named Regina to play her fearful reaction. Again, she and Mary Ellen withdrew to a corner of the room to watch the demon and Bonnie's flight reaction from a distance.

Like a scene from a play, Bonnie's inner struggle with her demon took shape before our eyes. The demon taunted her mercilessly and her reaction was to run. From the sidelines, Bonnie herself watched, wiping tears away and shaking her head. She said this struggle had been with her throughout her life.

"Is there anything familiar about this scene?" Cliff asked her. "Because I don't think you were born with this going on inside you. I think you learned this somewhere along the way. What does this remind you of? Who *are* these people?"

Wally and Regina had hardly begun to play their roles when Bonnie nodded, and Mary Ellen signaled them to stop. The demon was her dad, Bonnie said. He had berated Bonnie and her brothers and sisters constantly while they were growing up. Cliff asked who the part fleeing was, and Bonnie said that was her. Cliff asked how old she might have been when she first felt ridiculed by her dad, and she said at about age five.

RECOGNIZING THE SHADOW

I watched, completely absorbed. When I looked at Bonnie's demon, I saw my Editor. It had terrorized my childhood girlfriends just as Bonnie's demon had terrorized her. My Editor had terrorized me every time I tried to speak in a group or write a poem. When I looked at five-year-old Bonnie turning to flee from the demon, I saw myself leaving every group I had ever been a part of. I even saw myself leaving my creative writing behind when I couldn't bear the Editor's vicious criticism.

Bonnie had felt shame about having a demon inside her and about running from the demon instead of fighting back. She had felt so much shame about this inner struggle that she'd never been able to get much perspective on it before. She'd been caught between the terror and the flight with no way to stop the cycle. She had come to this workshop, where there were invisible arms to hold her while she got a good look at the demon and her reaction to it. Here, with this safety and support, she could see the struggle clearly enough that she could decide what to do about it.

I realized suddenly that I could decide to step out onto the rug and get a good look at my Editor. My body instantly reacted: my heart started pounding and my lungs seemed to stop working. Everybody in the room would see my Editor. They would find out how critical I could be. They might shrink in horror from someone as critical as me. I squashed the idea and tried to forget that I'd had it.

When Cliff and Mary Ellen asked Bonnie what she wanted to do to shut up the demon and get some rest, Bonnie pointed to Regina and said she wanted that part of her to push the demon out of the room.

Like a stage director taking over for one of the characters in her own play, Bonnie changed places with Regina. With Cliff's and Mary Ellen's careful choreography and two people holding her in a special way to prevent injury, Bonnie dug her toes into the rug and pushed herself forward. As a growl roared from her throat, the two people holding her allowed her to make gradual but steady progress across the room toward the door. Her anger was a whole-body experience, releasing the fury she had stored in her body years earlier when her dad berated her. In front of her, Wally went on ranting aggressively, but slowly backed up as she pushed forward. When he reached the door, he stepped through it and the door closed behind him. She was done!

The two people holding her released her and Bonnie stood free, panting and looking totally pumped. She clenched and unclenched her fists as if she'd never noticed she had fists before. Cliff and Mary Ellen talked to her for a minute about the new, pumped sensation inside her body. They helped her create a mental image of it so that she could access it again more easily in the future.

I had never seen anyone look so happy before. The group stood around her in a circle, applauding. Wally reentered the room, and she de-roled with him, meaning she and Wally exchanged statements that removed him from the role of demon.

ARMS OF THE ANGELS

The next person to step into the middle of the circle was a man with reddish hair. I'll call him Lyle. Lyle said he wanted to feel better about himself. His mother had been an actress who was the center of attention everywhere she went. Lyle's inner play had three characters. A mother figure dressed in flashy colors paraded around the room saying, "I'm the special one." A father figure stood by the door, dressed in camouflage. He was saying, "I can't compete. I might as well go." A sad young Lyle stood looking down at the floor, saying, "I just want to be loved."

When asked what he wanted to happen in the scene, Lyle said he wanted the young child to hear that he was okay. He said he couldn't imagine either of his parents ever saying it; that would have been too good to be true. It needed to come from someone else. He said he might be able to believe it if it came from an angel. Cliff suggested that he look around the room and choose someone to play an angel.

Lyle looked at me. I tried to make my face as impassive as I could, but inside I was begging to be chosen. When Lyle asked if I would be willing to play that part, I nodded and stood up, trying to appear as if this happened every day. But my insides were in an uproar. *He chose me! Does this mean I'm okay? Can I really help here? Can I, can I?* I wanted desperately to believe that I was good enough to play an angel. And I wanted to be seen as good enough in the eyes of the group.

My Editor was there, too, saying, "Who do you think you are, masquerading as an angel? You, who never does anything right?"

I tried not to listen.

Lyle said an angel would be up high and dressed in gold, so he stood me on a chair and draped gold lamé fabric around my shoulders.

When they asked Lyle what the angel would say, he paused. Mary Ellen suggested that he play the angel and show us what it would say. He took my place on the chair, with the gold fabric around his shoulders, and I stood where he had been, assuming the role of Lyle for him. He placed his hands on my head, and was silent for a moment, as if he were listening for words from inside.

Cliff, looking up at him, said softly, "Lyle is here, and he wants to know from you, an angelic being, that he's okay. Would you be willing to tell him that?"

Lyle, as the angel, began to speak, haltingly at first. He said he wanted me to know that I was okay and that even though I had been left alone as a child, I was very special, and I had been born for a very special, unique purpose. Though I knew these words were for Lyle and not for me, my eyes filled with tears.

We switched places again. Cliff whispered in my ear to ask if I remembered what Lyle had said well enough to repeat it. I nodded. Mary Ellen turned on some tender music as I stood on the chair and wrapped the gold fabric around my shoulders. I placed my hands on Lyle's head and repeated what the angel had said, word for word.

Lyle bowed his head. I couldn't see his face, but I felt him begin to shake. I realized he was crying silently, and tears again filled my own eyes. I would not have moved my hands for anything in the world, so the tears spilled over and ran down my cheeks. I felt the warmth of his head through my hands, and something more than heat. Something was reaching him through me, as if I were a conduit. I would never have dared believe that an angelic blessing could reach another person through me. I felt more worth as a person than I had ever felt before.

FOUR KINDS OF SHAME

After Lyle, a man named Karl stepped out onto the rug to figure out why he was always fighting with his teenage son. In his play, a bully pounded on a defenseless victim. Karl recognized it as a reenactment of his relationship with his own father. As a boy, Karl had meekly played the victim in the face of his father's bullying. Now his teenage son was doing the same thing—only now Karl was the bully.

After Karl, a woman named Olivia wanted to take better care of herself: get more rest, eat better, and so on. Her play had two parts: a mother who was halfway out the door, saying, "You're too much trouble," and a young Olivia reaching out arms of longing and saying, "Stay here with me."

By the end of the afternoon, so much had happened that I needed time to digest it. I felt full in a way I had never felt before, as if my mind couldn't absorb much more. I took a walk in the woods and found a small lake, where I sat on a log and stared at the water.

I had helped Lyle by playing his angel. Memories of helping people were flashing through my mind like a slide show: the time I had clutched my brother Lee tightly to help him mourn at the memorial service for a young boy; the time I had listened all night to my high school classmate, Sue, whose brother had just witnessed the killings at Kent State. I had even saved a young girl from drowning in a swimming pool. I had helped many people, I just hadn't been able to *see* that I had. Like Lyle, I had not been able to believe it. It had seemed too good to be true.

Something Cliff had said on Friday night came back to me: that each of the four parts of us feels shame a little differently. I realized I had seen all four kinds of shame that day. One kind looked like Bonnie fleeing from a demon, feeling fear. One kind looked like Lyle, unable to believe his parents thought him good enough, feeling unworthy and unlovable. One looked like Karl, powerless and angry in the face of his father's rage. One looked like Olivia, weeping with grief and longing for the mother who was abandoning her.

In each of the inner plays I had seen acted out, a big part was doing something to hurt a smaller part, and the smaller part reacted. Bonnie's demon terrorized her, and she fled in fear. Lyle's mother belittled him, and his self-esteem deflated like a burst bubble. Karl's father bullied him, and he accepted defeat. Olivia's mother left, and Olivia wept for her return.

Not only had I seen the four kinds of shame acted out that day, I had *felt* all four kinds of shame since arriving at the workshop, just as I did in my daily life.

Like Bonnie, I felt shame about having a critical Editor inside, so I fled from exposing it to the group. In my life, I ran from groups and from my own creativity as a writer.

Like Lyle, I felt shame about wanting to believe I was okay, so I wanted the group to see me as an angel. In my life, I starved myself of support, believing I didn't deserve it.

Like Karl, I felt shame about being powerless, so I didn't speak up to the man who took my seat. In my life, I felt powerless to get what I wanted.

Like Olivia, I felt shame about how I connected with people, so I felt uncomfortable getting long hugs and looked for comfort in a cup of tea rather than in the company of another person. In my life, I was too ashamed to play games with my daughter.

My box had four walls, and its outlines were becoming visible.

Chapter 4

Bouncing Off the Walls

As I sat by the lake, I thought about the battle I had waged with my Editor for so many years. I pictured myself hurling my body against a wall. The wall never budged, but I hurled myself at it anyway. Each time, I failed to make a mark on its hard, cruel facade and lay bruised at its feet. Each time it sneered at me, saying that I was too critical to belong or to have women friends, that I couldn't be trusted not to hurt people.

If, however, there were four kinds of shame, I wasn't up against a single wall. I was trapped inside a box with four walls. I had been bouncing off the four walls all along, without knowing it.

The first wall was my Editor, of course. It towered over me with a contemptuous grin. When I was in a group, it judged and shamed others.

The Editor Wall
"You never get it right!"

When I assumed the Editor's voice and blurted our judgmental, unkind things to others, only to see the pain I inflicted, the Editor judged and shamed me for hurting them. It told me there was something wrong with me. Even when I was alone, it judged me. It judged everything I thought, everything I wrote.

Its judgments hurt. When I couldn't take the hurt any more, I bounced to the next wall in the box.

The Angry Wall
"Just try harder!"

Then I felt angry. My angry self was an athletic coach pacing back and forth in front of a blackboard, screaming at the players who had failed to win the game.

"Just try harder!" the coach yelled, slamming one fist into the other. "Quitting is for weaklings! Just use *will power!* If that doesn't work, just focus on something else!"

"Just" was the coach's favorite word. When nothing worked, the coach threw the chalk on the floor in disgust. "You just can't do it, can you?! Just get out of here, then, I'm done with you!"

When the coach gave up, I felt like a failure, and that hurt. When I couldn't take the hurt any more, I bounced to the next wall in the box.

Now I felt sad. My sad self was a child sitting in a puddle, crying, hugging the pain to her chest. "You can't connect, so you're all alone," she said. "The loneliness hurts, but it's all you've got. You must never let it go."

The sadness felt overwhelming. When I couldn't take the sadness any more, I bounced to the next wall.

The Sad Wall
"I can't connect!"

I was up against the last wall, feeling hopeless and resigned. It was time to face the inevitable. My resigned self was sitting slump-shouldered in a sailboat with a slack sail. Not a breath of wind stirred. The sailor reminded me of Lyle looking down at the floor, wanting to be loved.

The Resigned Wall
"I guess I'm a _____"

"This boat has a name," the sailor said listlessly. She pointed to the prow of her boat, where the name *The Loner* had been painted in black letters. If I moved my head slightly, the name changed to *The Tomboy*, and if I moved it again, it became *The Intellectual.* The sailor had a label to explain what was happening. I was a loner who didn't like being with other people, or a tomboy who didn't enjoy the company of other girls, or an intellectual who had different interests than those of other women.

A NAME FOR THE BOX

The contemptuous editor, the bullying coach, the crying child, the becalmed sailor: these were the four walls of the box I came to call my Shaming-Fleeing box.

Trapped inside the box was the nine-year-old me who still wanted what she'd always wanted: to belong, like a puppy in a cozy, squirming heap of littermates. It was her yearning to belong that had propelled me back into group after group to give it one more try. She was the one who had been bouncing off these four walls all these years.

"I want to belong," she said. "Maybe if I try one more time, it will work!"

"You'll never belong," sneered the Editor. "You're too critical."

"That sounds bad," said the nine-year-old. "I feel ashamed."

"You *should* feel ashamed," said the Editor. "You can't be trusted not to hurt people."

"Me, want to hurt people? Not *me*!" *Bounce.*

"If talking is the problem, then just stop talking!" shouted the coach.

"But it's so frustrating," said the nine-year-old. "Something always blurts out!"

"Just try harder," the coach clamored. "Use *will power*!"

"It doesn't work!" said the nine-year-old. "I just get angry, and then it leaks out even worse."

"Just focus on something else!" hammered the coach. "Just take your mind off it!"

"But something always leaks out!" cried the nine-year-old. "This doesn't work!"

"I'm done with you!" fumed the coach. "Just get out of here!"

"I feel like a failure, and it hurts," said the nine-year-old. *Bounce.*

"You can't connect," said the child crying in the puddle. "But no matter how much it hurts, you have to hold on and never let it go."

"But it hurts!" said the nine-year-old. *Bounce.*

"It's hopeless," said the sailor with a shrug. "It's time you faced the facts about yourself. You're a tomboy, a loner, an intellectual—that's why you don't belong."

"But I want to belong!" cried the nine-year-old. *Bounce.*

"But you don't, do you?" jeered the Editor. "Because you're so critical!" *Bounce.*

"Just be quiet!" yelled the coach. "Just try harder! Just focus!" *Bounce.*

"You can't connect," cried the child, "you're alone." *Bounce.*

"Read my lips: it's hopeless," said the sailor, pointing at the boat's prow. *Bounce.*

The nine-year-old inside the box wanted to belong. And she went right on wanting and wanting and wanting.

THINKING OUTSIDE THE BOX

In rare moments of clarity through the years, I had seen that I was stuck in a cycle. I called it "going around and around in my head." That's when I tried jumping out of the box.

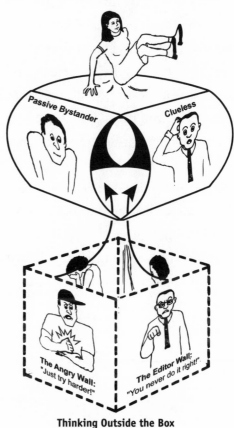

And every time I did, it suddenly felt as if I were in a whole new world. There was a fresh breeze blowing through the house! But the box wasn't gone. It had simply turned inside out. Each wall had become its mirror opposite.

The Editor became clueless, scratching its head with a vacant expression. "Gee, maybe you've been thinking about this all wrong. Maybe you've never really had any trouble

Thinking Outside the Box

being in a group!" Clueless was the one who decided, when I read the magazine article about friendships, to set up the new mom-and-tot group.

"Groups are great!" said the clueless one. "No problem!"

Turned inside out, the box's angry wall became a passive bystander. "Hey, this is going to be easy," said the bystander. "Just say anything that pops into your head!" The bystander imposed no rules. Inane, phony—it didn't matter what I said or did.

Inside out, the box's sad wall became stoic. "Feelings get in the way," said the stoic, its face like stone. "You don't need feelings to make friends; in fact, it's easier without them."

When the box turned inside out, the slump-shouldered sailor in a becalmed boat became a driven go-getter. She wasn't going to let a little thing like no breeze slow her down! Where the sailor had told me to face facts, the go-getter told me to ignore them. "What we need here is positive thinking!" she crowed. "You can be a different person. All you have to do is snap your fingers. Problem solved!"

With a box made of clueless, the bystander, the stoic and the go-getter, I had been no more able to make friends than before. The box had turned inside out, but nothing had really changed. Eventually the box snapped back into its original shape, and life went back to the way it had been.

Why had nothing changed? Because, as it turned out, the box existed for very good reasons, and those reasons hadn't changed.

Chapter 5

⚬⚭⚬

Reasons for a Box

As the sun set over the lake, I got up and walked back through the woods. I wondered why I had a box like this. Did everyone have one?

Back in the workshop room, I looked around me at the other participants. Some of them, mingling happily and talking in small groups, obviously thrived in groups. Others, like me, hovered around the edges, avoiding contact until the last possible moment.

Maybe, I thought, *I should ask myself the question that Cliff had asked Bonnie: What does this remind you of?* If she wasn't born with the demon and the impulse to flee from it inside her, maybe I wasn't born with my Editor and the impulse to flee from groups either. Maybe I had learned them somewhere along the way.

Had I seen them somewhere before? I asked myself. Had I ever known anyone who wanted friends but criticized them? Who avoided groups and sat quietly when in one?

I could hardly believe I had never thought of it before. My father!

DAD'S FRIEND GEORGE

I rarely saw Dad with friends as I was growing up. But then, he was a breadwinner with a wife and five children and had little spare time. He sometimes talked about the men he worked with, but I don't remember them coming to our house. Only once do I remember going to one of theirs, to the home of Dad's friend, Dave von Gillern. Dave had a huge model train layout in his basement. It had tracks running not only around a big table in the center of the room, but also along rows of narrow shelves on each wall, and even across the back of the basement door.

Occasionally Mom and Dad invited another couple from the church over for an evening of bridge. One such couple was a man named George and his wife. George was a slender, rather fragile looking man with a nervous laugh. Over the bridge table, Dad talked and laughed with George as if they were buddies. When the evening was over, however, and George and his wife had gone home, I heard Dad talking about him to my mother in a very different way.

"What a jackass George is," Dad said contemptuously.

When Dad criticized, he spoke through clenched teeth, as if he were a dog tearing the meat off a bone. That's how he talked about George.

"With that silly smile of his," Dad said, "I'm almost embarrassed to have him over to the house."

My stomach felt a little bit sick when I heard Dad talk about George that way. It didn't feel right.

Dad and George once went on a hunting trip together, during which George accidentally shot himself in the foot. As Dad told us the story later, George hopped around on one foot while the other foot was bleeding from the gunshot. Dad laughed so hard his ears turned red and his eyes watered.

Now, as I remembered Dad's hunting story, I realized his behavior was similar to mine with my girlfriends: ridiculing, even contemptuous of them, laughing while they were hurting.

THE TRAUMA OF WAR

During World War II, Dad fought with the Marines' Sixth Division in the South Pacific. He saw a lot of combat and came home with two Purple Hearts.

For forty years, Dad didn't say much about the War. It wasn't until the late 1980s that he opened up about his Marine experience to my younger brother Lee, who had become interested in knowing more. Lee first researched the battles in which Dad had participated and formulated specific questions to jog Dad's memory. He then did a series of interviews with Dad on tape and shared the tapes with the rest of us. When I listened to them, I heard for the first time about the kind of horrors Dad had seen, and it helped me understand him better. There were a hundred questions I wanted to ask, but within a few months Dad was gone.

While I was growing up, there was at times an almost tangible cloud of some unnamed matter around Dad. I realize now it was trauma. As I've studied trauma and post-traumatic stress disorder (PTSD), I've come to see many of their symptoms in Dad's behavior. He criticized us, just as he criticized George, and to our faces. I walked on eggshells when I was around him because I feared a verbal attack. When Dad first returned from the South Pacific, my mother told me recently, he avoided large bushes like rhododendrons because they reminded him of the jungle and there might be someone hiding behind them. Dad walked on eggshells sometimes, too.

During Dad's interviews with Lee, he said that he had been terribly shy, introverted and anti-social in high school. "I have never been a joiner," he said.

But he had made friends in the Marines, and he spoke of them on the tapes with real affection. His closest friend was a man named Maynard Cleon Barsness from Minnesota, whose last name came right after Dad's in the alphabet, so they often stood next to each other in line. Barsness was killed in action during the battle of Okinawa, while Dad was in a hospital recovering from a blast concussion. Dad wrote to his mother regularly from the Pacific but rarely mentioned casualties because he didn't want to worry her. But he wrote to her about Barsness.

"A guy's luck, even mine, can't last forever," he wrote. "Barsness and I thought we were immune to such stuff, but Barsness is gone and I am left by myself now. He was the closest buddy I ever had, he was as close if not closer to me than [my brother] Jim is. I'm not ashamed to say I cried many nights after it happened. I wish I'd get a case of amnesia or something, for a guy's memory can just about drive him nuts at times."

One common symptom of PTSD is the inability to stop the memory of a painful event from repeating in your mind. Other common symptoms include survivor guilt, irritability, hypersensitivity to noise, emotional numbing, and withdrawal from relationships.

Another of Dad's friends, a corporal from Texas named Raymond Hugo Gollnick, was killed on Okinawa right in front of him. A few of the men were taking a cigarette break, lounging on a rock pile. A Japanese soldier appeared out of nowhere, took aim at the first Marine he saw—who happened to be Gollnick—and shot him through the head before disappearing down a hole. The Japanese had dug networks of underground tunnels on the island, and the Marines quickly found the entrance to a vertical shaft among the rocks. They threw in concussion grenades and other explosives, but it was too late for Gollnick. Although there was nothing he could have done to save his friend's life, Dad blamed himself for not reacting quickly enough, and I could still hear the remorse in his voice forty years later.

Dad was skilled with a rifle and survived where many of his fellow Marines did not, though he attributed his survival largely to luck and his ability to keep his wits about him under fire. He was promoted to sergeant and had not only his own survival to worry about, but the survival of his men.

On Okinawa, he once had to order his platoon to open fire on a native man who was scrambling up the side of a ravine to get away from them. The risk was too great that the man might be a lookout for the Japanese. Dad's men had been under terrible stress for weeks, with little to shoot at or to do. When he gave the command to shoot at the islander, he saw the ground around the man explode in a circle ten feet wide. When the man's body was searched, they found he had probably been scrounging for souvenirs to sell. At the time, Dad had seen no choice but to shoot, but forty years later, he knew that the incident had stuck in his mind because it had been his decision to fire.

At dusk on the island of Guam, when it was time to dig in for the night, the Marines would walk forward from their position, shooting from the hip without aiming. They carpeted the undergrowth with a barrage of bullets to ensure that no enemy soldiers lay in hiding. They would dig their foxholes and then, when darkness came, retreat several hundred yards and dig new foxholes to sleep in. When the Japanese counterattacked during the night, they would attack the advance position, not knowing the Marines were no longer there.

The war was long over, but its effect on Dad impacted the entire family. Living with Dad was like living under a barrage of criticism. He had no idea about how to be a father to five kids, and he hated the job he drove to every day. But here he was, dug in for the night with all these mouths to feed.

There are photos in our family albums that show another side of Dad: the shy young father nervously holding an infant in his skinny arms with a look of awed wonder. I think that after losing people at close range in war, he was afraid to get close to us. He found it easier to retreat behind a barrage of criticism than to risk close connections—connections that could be taken from him just as his Marine friends had been taken.

A PAINFUL BOND

For years I felt so much shame about criticizing my friends that I had never noticed this similarity with my father. It had never occurred to me that I might have had a *reason* for being so critical. The very best kind of reason, in fact: I loved my father. He was an irritable, critical man, but I loved him anyway. I didn't know he'd been hurt by the War. I didn't know that fathers weren't supposed to criticize their children. I loved him because he was my dad.

So I learned to do what he did, to criticize friends and to laugh while they hurt. If that's what my dad did, it must be the right thing to do. Criticism was a bond between us. The bond was a painful one, but my father didn't know how to connect with his children, and I preferred a painful bond to no bond at all.

That bond gave me something else as well, something crucial to my sense of self. It gave me the experience of loving someone. Loving painfully, yes, but loving all the same. Loving someone despite his imperfections, despite even his cruelty. Loving Dad was painful, but I preferred a painful way of loving to none at all.

Thus was born the Editor, an internalized version of my father's voice, criticizing me the way he'd always done. In order to deal with my Editor, I would have to risk breaking that bond with my father and losing all connection with him. I would also have to risk feeling that I wasn't a loving person after all.

These risks were the real reason that I was unable to change the pattern all those years. When I was with a group of friends, my painful bond with my father prevented me from having a healthy bond with my friends. I was "belonging," as I so longed to do, but it was with Dad I belonged, not with friends my own age. By internalizing my father as the Editor, I had a painful connection with him rather than a healthy connection with my friends.

Chapter 6

Dad's Own Box

I lay on my bed in the bunkhouse that evening, staring up at the wooden beams that crisscrossed the ceiling. As I thought about what I knew of my dad's life, I realized that he'd had a box very like mine.

Dad worked for more than forty years in a white-collar job with few opportunities for creative expression. Yet he was undoubtedly a creative man. In the evening after work, he frequently stole away to his workshop in the basement to carve objects from wood and make furniture. He was an inventor at heart and created various gadgets for the household.

Dad did not suffer fools gladly and was quick to point out imperfections in his children. The same perfectionism showed in his woodworking, too. When he bought a tool, he bought the best one available. And he held himself to the same high standard. In fact, although he was a hard worker, I don't remember ever seeing him look unkempt. I recognize now the signs of an Editor in him that attacked his own imperfections as well as ours.

Although Dad could act grandiose at times, I think his shyness was an indication of how small he felt inside. As a young man he had been terribly skinny. In old photographs, his clothes hung off him as if he were barely able to hold them up. When I listened to his stories about the War, I heard a man trying hard to be big enough to meet its challenges and reveling in occasional opportunities to show his "clout," as when a church member who was a Navy Captain paid him a call in front of his friends.

Later in life, he took up nature photography, specializing in close-ups of wildflowers. He told me the trick was to find a perfect specimen, unharmed by weather or insects. The blossoms he captured on film were as fragile as he was inside.

Dad rarely did anything playful with his children. I remember sitting with him in church. He was bored by the sermon and I was too young to understand it. He removed his gold-color tie clasp and playfully moved it towards me, opening and closing its jaws as if it were a tiny alligator. I was delighted, of course, and grinned up at him, but he suddenly froze and stopped. He withdrew his hand and put the clasp back on his necktie.

When I picture the jaws of that tie clasp chomping playfully at me, I see also the jaws of my hand critter opening wide to sing for my daughter in the bathtub. And I see both of us freezing and stopping short.

Like me, Dad had a "bad back" and costly dental bills. He felt uncomfortable hugging people. I believe he was terrified of death, as I was, but he preferred to deny his fear. He was fond of telling me that he was going to outlive all of us.

I remember sitting next to him at the age of five or six while he watched a war movie on television. He sat in a wicker chair, a beer in one hand, and stared stonily at the screen. I sat on the floor beside him, looking alternately at the television and at his face.

With my own daughter, I had reenacted this scene many times, sinking in leaden silence into the sofa while my daughter sat alone nearby.

In talking with Dad's sisters after he died, I learned that their mother, my grandmother, had been emotionally unavailable to Dad at a formative age. When he was a toddler, Grandma had given birth to stillborn twins, and she withdrew from her two older boys in shock and grief. During the War, Dad wrote of a favorite fantasy in a letter home. It was a fantasy in which he was lying in bed and drinking through a tube from a bathtub full of fresh milk suspended from the ceiling above him. A vivid image indeed of a man craving a mother's nourishment and support.

Chapter 7

Motivation to Change

The workshop ended Sunday at noon and I drove home, a jumble of thoughts and feelings. I had witnessed so much. I had seen people stepping out of boxes they'd been trapped in their whole lives. I had seen them arrive feeling ashamed and depart feeling good about themselves. I had seen them discovering that they'd been loving instead of cold, wise instead of foolish, strong instead of weak, faithful instead of faithless.

With so much stirring inside me, I felt more alive than I had felt in a long time. My feelings had awakened. There seemed to be rivers of fear, anger, sadness, shame, guilt, and joy streaming through me. I had hugged Cliff before leaving, had been able to hold onto him a little longer, and felt good about myself for having done so. I had so much to think about, it was as if there were flashbulbs going off inside my brain, lighting up all the dark corners.

I was aware of many things I wanted to change about myself. In fact, I felt pretty "screwed up," as I named it to myself. I saw myself as a person with whole chunks of herself that needed rescuing from boxes. I pictured the list running down my left arm, "a list as long as my arm," I said aloud to myself in the car. The future looked exhilarating . . . and terrifying, and a little overwhelming.

I already felt better about myself than I had in years. I had actually participated in a group and not come away thinking of myself as a terrible person.

IMPACT AT HOME

Over the following weeks, I looked at my life with new eyes. My closet was full of clothes that were black, gray, and dark blue. I owned no dancing shoes, no sexy underwear, no flashy earrings.

My daughter had just started fifth grade and her new school picture arrived. When I looked at it, I felt as if I were seeing her for the first time. She was smiling nervously. She looked unsure of herself, almost as if she were afraid someone was going to hit her.

Before I left for the workshop, she had been collecting centipedes and other bugs in our backyard for a science project. To my amazement and secret pride, she enjoyed watching these creepy-crawly creatures and even let them run over her hand. The very thought gave me the shivers. I had never seen anything fun or attractive about bugs, and as a child I'd had a real phobia of spiders.

A week or two after I arrived home, my daughter found a spider in her room and came running to me in fear, asking me to kill it. I had never known her to be afraid of spiders before. If I hadn't attended the workshop, I might not have thought anything of it. I might even have felt a guilty pride that she was afraid of spiders just as I had been at her age, that she was definitely her mother's daughter.

But now, the more I looked at her through new eyes, the more I saw her building boxes like mine. Just as I had built my Shaming-Fleeing box so I could be like my dad, she was building boxes so she could be like her mom: lacking in self-assurance, scared of insects—scared of life.

She had always made friends easily, a skill I had often admired. Would that change, too, I wondered? Would she become scared of groups and unable to bond with other girls her age?

I had a sudden vision of boxes getting passed from parent to child, down the generations, inexorably, until someone finally said, "No! It stops here, with me."

My view of parenting began to change. Where before I had met my own and my husband's needs first, I instead began to place her needs first. At the age of ten, her greatest need was to have a physically and emotionally healthy mother who could support her as she became a woman. A mother who could serve as a positive role model, and not as the blueprint for depression and despair. In order for that to happen, I would need to change. I felt thankful that I had witnessed firsthand during the workshop that change can leave you feeling good about yourself, not bad.

As I began to tackle that list as long as my arm, remembering my daughter's need for a healthy mom was a vital source of motivation. Whenever I faced an issue that looked too dark, too awful to admit to myself, I had only to think, *this could help my daughter,* and all the motivation I needed to face it was right there to help me.

With one major exception, that is. It took three years for me to get the courage to confront the Editor.

Chapter 8

Kittens in a Litter

W hen a cat has a litter of kittens, sometimes the biggest kitten isn't the first to be born.

There was so much I wanted in my life, and I wanted it so urgently, that I put myself on a kind of fast track. In November of that year, I went to Memphis, Tennessee to attend a second workshop—this time as a full participant. Three months later I went to a women's retreat called the Woman Within Initiation and, with other women who had attended, became part of a women's group that met weekly. I began seeing a therapist and integrating into my daily life the changes that were happening inside me. The following September I went back to the A-frame in the woods for a third workshop, this time bringing my husband with me. Over that weekend, I realized I wanted to become a facilitator and began adding trainings and practice sessions to my schedule, and adding a career change to my long-term goals.

As I examined each scene of my inner play and empowered or blessed some young part of me, the Editor waited in the wings.

Whenever I became aware of its presence, I was filled with fear and loathing, and I shrank from exposing it to others. After years of avoiding groups, I was beginning to feel I might belong in the warm, accepting, invisible arms I found at every workshop and training. How could I show the people in these groups how critical I could be? Surely they would shun me and send me away. I had waited too long for this; I couldn't take the risk of ruining it all.

Looking back at what I gained from those earliest workshops, I see myself preparing the way for what came later. I gradually removed my fear about being in groups, built a support system to help me as I grew, and acquired some basic tools.

GETTING MY VOICE BACK

The workshop in Memphis is where I did my first Shadow Work process, facilitated by a married couple there because Cliff thought it best that my first experience of Shadow Work not be led by a family member. For the first time I saw one of my inner bad guys played by another person, and at first, I couldn't even speak back to it.

This bad guy was not the Editor but a less complicated figure: a bully, smacking one hand with his fist, and yelling angrily. It was the athletic coach who had been yelling at me to stay quiet inside my head for years, who had told me just be quiet, just try harder, just focus on something else. My reaction to the bully was not fear, as it was with the Editor, but a feeling of powerlessness. I directed a woman named Denise, who was playing me as a girl, to kneel before the bully and cover her mouth with her right hand. All I wanted was to get my voice back.

When the facilitators asked me if this scene was familiar, I realized the bully was another side of Dad that I had internalized. It was the domineering Dad who cared most about his own needs, who yelled at us to be quiet, and who gave us the message that he wished we weren't around.

I had grown up feeling that I had no right to talk back or to question authority. I didn't even feel I had a right to take up space in the world. The young me played by Denise felt powerless and ashamed. This scene between the bully and the self-stifler had been the source of my anger and my shame during that first workshop when the man with the military haircut took my seat.

Another realization came to me as I looked at the scene. When I looked at Denise with her hand over her mouth, I saw not only myself as a girl, but my mother stifling her anger towards my father, and probably towards her own father as well. I felt sure I had learned this stifle response from her.

Stifling my anger had worked when I was a child, but it wasn't working for me any more. In order to go further in my training, I had to be able to speak up, ask questions, ask for what I needed. I needed to have my voice back. When the workshop facilitators asked me what I wanted to do with this inner play between the bully and the little girl stifling herself, I thought about Bonnie. She had pushed her demon out of the room. I didn't care about the bully leaving the room. I just wanted him to shut up. My anger seemed to reside in my throat and I wanted to shout back at the bully until *he* was the one getting stifled.

Because I had never allowed myself to shout at the top of my lungs before, the facilitators put on some loud music so I wouldn't feel self-conscious. Two people held me in the safety hold, allowing me to dig my feet into the carpet and feel angry with my whole body without injuring myself or anyone else.

I started shouting back at the bully, while the group enthusiastically cheered me on.

"Go for it! You can do it! Tell him!" they shouted.

Yelling felt good at first, but after about a minute, I had stopped for some reason. I was arguing instead, trying to reason with the bully, and I was getting nowhere.

The facilitators asked me if there was a risk for me to silence the bully once and for all and get my voice back. The room was suddenly quiet. Someone had switched off the music.

I nodded in surprise. Yes, there was a risk! I was fiercely liberal and had been an anti–nuclear power activist for a brief time in college. I had attended demonstrations and committed civil disobedience, even going to prison once for a few days. If I got my voice back, I might speak out in a way that so infuriated my opponents or the government, they would silence me for good—they would have me killed.

The risk certainly made a lot of sense: nobody would want to get killed for speaking out! As we talked, I realized that I had feared getting killed by Dad as a child. There were times when I had felt his anger seething beneath the surface like lava beneath a volcano. His anger felt very big, big enough to bring the world to an end. Even when he was just a bit irritable, I tread softly for fear of arousing his anger. I realized that when I had said he'd given us the message that he didn't want us around, what I had really meant was that he wished we were dead. I thought again about my father's time in the Marines. He had been trained as a killer and somehow his ability to kill, and perhaps his experience of combat, had come through into his family life.

What a good idea, the facilitators said, to stifle myself and not risk getting killed! I had never thought of it as a strategy before. I had thought that I was just too cowardly to talk back or speak out against authority. I thought of it as something shameful, as something wrong with me.

The facilitators went on to ask if not getting my voice back was keeping me from getting killed. Or did I ever get killed anyway, even if it was just getting killed inside my head?

The answer surprised me. Yes! During those darkest hours when I thought about suicide, I had imagined myself dead many times. And in a sense, the bullying athletic coach had even been "killing" me by killing my voice in groups all these years. Clearly, I was getting killed anyway, so I might as well take the risk to get my voice back.

"I'm willing to take the risk," I said. The moment I said the words, I felt like yelling again. In an instant, the music was back on and my voice rose in volume. I dug my feet into the carpet and yelled for all I was worth. The group had come to its feet and was cheering loudly. My body was releasing anger and frustration that I had kept trapped inside for years.

When my anger reached its peak, the facilitators signaled the man playing the bully to gradually sink to the floor and become silent. The two people holding me let go and I stood free, my feet firmly planted on the floor, breathing hard.

I had won! I couldn't remember ever having felt truly victorious before, and it was an incredible rush. I felt a new power in my throat. When the facilitators asked what it was like, I described it as a red ball of fire. They invited me to close my eyes and feel the red ball of fire in my throat. Did it have a message for me?

Yes, it did!

It said, "I can speak."

THE IMPACT

For a few days I was hoarse from the yelling, but I had my voice back. Over the weeks that followed, I felt a new capability inside to speak up for myself, whether it was to reclaim my seat cushion at a workshop or ask for a raise at work. When I tried to tell people what the new capability felt like, though, I found it difficult to describe.

Something Cliff had said that first weekend came back to me: the four parts of the self are like portals we can step through to reach our highest potential. When I spoke up instead of stifling myself, it felt as if a doorway had opened in what had previously been a solid wall, and through the doorway came a cool, bracing breeze. Now that my body had a sensation to match it, the idea of portals made sense.

The doorway was my Warrior portal. Shouting the bully down had opened the doorway to my Warrior self, who was my voice for speaking truth to power, my strength for doing battle against powerlessness and depression, my integrity that took responsibility for my physical and emotional well-being, and my courage for facing the difficult tasks ahead. I had a stronger sense of myself, as if I stood on more solid ground and a thicker line had been drawn around me in the soil at my feet. I pictured my Warrior drawing that line with a sword. I knew, with a Warrior's good sense, that I had a right to exist and to take up space.

I felt a thrill as I realized this portal was only one of four. An image came to me of a pavilion with lofty doorways facing north, south, east and west. I could step through each doorway in turn and reach new worlds beyond. The future looked more hopeful than it had in years.

When I shouted the bully down and found the red ball of fire in my throat, the scene inside me changed. I no longer had a bully berating a defenseless victim. I had an assertive self asking for what I needed and taking responsibility for maintaining what I had.

Because the scene inside me had changed, my outward behavior changed as well. I spoke up in groups and questioned what didn't make sense to me. I took better care of my back and my teeth and spent less money on doctors. I wrote essays, book reviews, and letters to politicians. I opened up to people and kept a daily journal for the first time in years. The size of my journal grew from 29 pages for 1996 to an impressive 380 pages for 1997.

Chapter 9

Finding Support

I attended the Woman Within Initiation in February, 1996, seeking to build a support network of women friends. I knew I had a lot of work before me and I wanted help getting through the dark nights of the soul I knew lay ahead. I had been having nights like that for years and no longer wanted to spend them thinking about suicide.

I knew that, as an initiation weekend, Woman Within was structured quite differently from the workshops I had attended thus far. But I knew from a friend who had gone through it herself that I would have an opportunity to draw out a scene from my inner play and take action to change it.

My inner play looked like a birthing room, with my infant self struggling to be born from the womb of the Great Mother, the Divine Feminine. Through an opening in the circle of women, I crawled on my belly as the group urged me on. On through the birth channel, formed by the stomachs of women on their hands and knees, I struggled into the open and into the welcoming arms of a woman playing the role of midwife.

As I lay resting, looking into the faces of the women surrounding me, I heard a female voice say, "You are not alone." The voice came not from anyone in the room but from somewhere inside me, yet it was as audible as if it had been spoken aloud. It frightened me. I tried not to think about what it meant. I was still an atheist, and I had no way to explain it. In the months that followed, I tried to push away the memory of hearing that inexplicable voice.

Not until a year later was I ready to admit to myself whose voice I had heard. It was on a dark day when despair had taken over. As I lit a candle and set it next to me, I felt a presence, as of a woman with strong, loving arms. I knew that her voice was the one I had heard, and that she was Divine. She was letting me know that I was not now, and never had been, alone.

Like my father, who had visualized drinking milk from a bathtub suspended from the ceiling, I longed to believe in something greater than myself and to be nurtured body and soul by it. When I allowed myself to acknowledge that longing, and the possibility of that longing being met, I began turning away from atheism. My Sovereign portal to a life of spirituality had opened just a crack. Before long, I was to fling it wide open.

ADDICTED TO SHAME

In the months that followed, I came to the seemingly bizarre conclusion that I was addicted to shame. I didn't want to be. I wanted to accept myself. If I had to be addicted to something, I preferred to be addicted to blessing.

In September, 1996, when I returned to the A-frame in the woods with my husband for another Shadow Work workshop, that's what I asked for: to be addicted to blessing. I expected others not to know what I was talking about. To my surprise, most the people in the room nodded in understanding.

My inner play unfolded to reveal a small, listless part of me saying, "I'm not good enough." Nearby stood the Editor, supplying the shame I was addicted to, telling me I never did anything right. The listless part reminded me of the slump-shouldered sailor sitting in the sailboat with a slack sail. She had resigned herself to believing what the Editor told her.

When the facilitators asked me what the listless part needed, I said she needed a blessing. I wanted to hear that I was okay just the way I was, and this listless girl was the part of me who needed to hear it. The one I really wanted to hear it from was the Editor, meaning my Dad, but I couldn't imagine Dad ever saying it. The facilitators asked if I would like to hear it from an Ideal Dad instead. I had never heard of an Ideal Dad before, but I leapt at the chance to meet one. I chose a tall, stately man named Tim to play the Ideal Dad. I indicated where he should stand, some distance away from the listless part, and there he stood, waiting for his lines.

The facilitators asked me what qualities an Ideal Dad has.

"He's understanding," I answered, "and compassionate, and loving."

They asked me if *I* would be willing to play that role myself, and be understanding and compassionate and loving toward the sad, listless part of me.

I was willing, yes, but was I capable? Could I give myself a blessing? It seemed almost too good to be true. Then I remembered Lyle. Something angelic had come to him through me. Maybe this time something angelic could come to *me*.

As I changed places with Tim and took on the role of Ideal Dad,

I spoke haltingly at first. Some tender music was playing, and that helped me get started. I looked at Tim, who was the small, listless part of me that felt she wasn't good enough. I told her I loved her exactly the way she was, and that I would always be there to help.

Suddenly, I couldn't stand being so distant from that part of myself. I stepped forward and knelt in front of Tim and put my arms around him. I held Tim as I would have held my daughter. I told that sad, listless part of myself what I had always wanted to hear from my own father: that I was fine the way I was. I told her I would always be there for support. I stroked Tim's hair, kissed his forehead, and told him I loved him. But it was not Tim I was holding and speaking endearments to, it was the part of myself that Tim was portraying.

When I had finished, Tim and I switched places. Tim knelt before me and put his arms around me. He held me and told me I was fine the way I was. He stroked my hair and kissed my forehead and told me he loved me. But it was not Tim who was holding me, it was a long denied part of myself blessing me.

My mind wandered off. I found myself thinking about what I would do at the end of the day. Should I go for a walk before dinner, or maybe afterwards? My face must have changed.

Was there a risk, the facilitators asked, for me to let in this blessing?

Yes, and how ironic! I had longed for a blessing like this. When I finally had the opportunity to receive it, it felt so risky. If I let the blessing in, the risk was that it might go away again and I might give up hope.

The risk certainly made a lot of sense. I had lived for twenty years believing there was no God and no meaning in life, and that the things I most wanted were too good to be true. My new belief was as fragile as a young seedling, and to lose it now would indeed feel like giving up hope. The facilitators asked, Was my not receiving this blessing keeping me from giving up hope, or did I ever give up hope anyway?

I realized that I gave up hope all the time! What was I doing when I thought of suicide but giving up hope? I decided I might as well take the risk to let this blessing in.

Tim repeated the lines I had spoken. When he told me I was fine the way I was and that he would always be there for support, I started to cry. He stroked my hair and kissed my forehead and told me he loved me. I cried more deeply. He held me and rocked me until my crying stopped.

It felt wonderful beyond imagining to hear a blessing like this and be able to receive it. I felt a warm glow inside my chest. It seemed made of gold, like the sun. As Tim gradually pulled away, I closed my eyes and asked internally if this warm glow made of gold like the sun had something to say to me about me.

I am lovable, was the answer.

I had found a source of blessing inside myself, where I could never lose it again. This source felt quite different from the cool, bracing breeze coming through my Warrior portal. This was like sunlight pouring through a doorway and soaking into the floorboards. This doorway was my Sovereign portal to self-acceptance. Letting the blessing in had opened the doorway to my Sovereign self, who could let in the support and nurture of a network of friends. My Sovereign was my self-acceptance even when I made mistakes, my vision of a happier life, my mission to heal myself and others, my belief in life.

I was still in a sailboat, but my experience of it was completely different. I basked on the sunlit deck of a seagoing craft, and all was peaceful and serene. I was lovable the way I was. I was lovable even if the boat never moved another inch. I envisioned a very different life for myself, in which many things I had once thought too good to be true—including a career helping people—were within my grasp. I could fill my days with activities I felt passionate about. I wasn't meant to go it alone at all. I deserved support and found it there for the asking. I felt a compassion for myself that I had never known was possible and quickly found a corresponding compassion for others as well.

Over the months that followed, I kept in touch with the people I had met at these workshops and developed friendships with the women I knew from my Woman Within initiation weekend. My network had more men friends than women in it at first, and most of the men lived in other states, but at least I had a list of people to reach out to when I was feeling down. I no longer needed or wanted to starve myself of support.

Before long, the sunlight had heated the water's surface beneath my little boat, and a gentle breeze began to flutter its sails. My next step would turn the breeze into a gale-force wind.

Chapter 10

Facing the Editor

With a voice and the beginnings of a support network, I now began training in earnest to become a facilitator, and to look further back into my childhood. I wanted to understand myself better and find the origins of the issues that were causing me so much unhappiness.

The Editor still waited in the wings. Occasionally in a workshop, when I watched someone else face their own version of the Editor, I felt terrified and ashamed. Sometimes a memory came to me when I stepped out onto the carpet and drew out a scene from my inner play. I remembered Dad picking on me, ridiculing me, making sarcastic remarks that stung. I discovered that I had lived in fear for so much of my life that I had never really thought about it. Fear had always been a given, a constant. For me the fear was symbolized by the swords that lived in our attic.

Dad had brought two Japanese swords home from the South Pacific, where he and his men had killed the soldiers who wore them.

One of the swords had a bullet hole through the blade. One of the memories that surfaced was of a dream I once had about the swords.

In my dream, the swords descended through the ceiling of our living room, their smooth, curved blades crossed at an angle. They stopped a few feet above my small back as I cowered, face down on the floor. Their cold, gray steel glinted in the light of a green lamp. The steel shafts disappeared into hilts bound with strips of dark cloth the color of dried blood.

In my dream, I wore a thin pink bathrobe made of synthetic fabric. It was the kind of bathrobe that didn't keep you warm; it merely covered up your pajamas so that your underpants would not show so much. My pajamas had flowers on them, and the flowers showed faintly through the bathrobe. They were the color of fading rosebuds.

As the swords descended, I pressed my face into my hands, afraid to look at death. The backs of my hands pressed into our living room rug with its pattern of maze-like squares. The rug's fibers imprinted their pattern on my skin.

I wasn't shaking. In an odd way, it was almost a relief that the swords had become visible. I had felt their presence every minute. If you have to die, it's better if you have a chance to prepare yourself. I was kneeling on a spot where an armchair usually sat. Beside me was a table on which my father played chess. The table top was made of maple. Dad had removed the original top and built a larger one, inlaid with squares of light and dark wood to use as a chessboard.

There were maple trees in the yard around our house. I loved one of them in particular, one near my bedroom window. I always imagined it sheltering the roof over me. A piece of maple had been chopped into little squares to make my father's chessboard.

The chessmen weren't on the board now, in my dream. In their coffin-shaped wooden box with the sliding lid, they lay hidden on a shelf below the tabletop. I knelt there and waited for the blow that could come at any moment.

I didn't move. My back was as still as the roof of our house, which was there to protect us from objects that might drop from the sky. My back wanted to protect me from the swords as they descended, but it would not be able to, not when Dad took shape before me, his hands on their hilts, ready to slice his daughter into pieces.

LOOKING LIKE THE BAD GUY

At a workshop in 1998, the time finally came for me to face the Editor. What it took, finally, was a willingness to look like the kind of "bad guy" who could carve up a little girl with swords.

To own the bad guy in myself, I had to admit to myself the many mean, critical, shaming comments I had made over the years that I would rather have forgotten. I had to own that I had inside me a figure who sliced and diced other people just as the Editor sliced and diced me inside my head.

The unpleasant truth was that I had already been looking like the bad guy to myself for years. I left groups of women friends believing I couldn't be trusted not to hurt people. In order to take the next step, I had to admit to myself that I was already experiencing what I most feared: looking like the bad guy. There was no longer any point in trying to avoid it.

When I felt ready, I stepped out onto the carpet and said, "I want to be creative."

I had been working as a technical writer for twelve years. I longed to write a story, a poem, maybe even a play—anything that wasn't strictly technical. The creative part of me sat in a chair at a desk, facing north. I wasn't sure why the desk had to face north until I remembered that the desk in my childhood room had faced north.

"I want to create," this part said, staring at blankness. Her voice was passive, unemotional. I asked a woman named Sylvia to play her and draped her in shiny green.

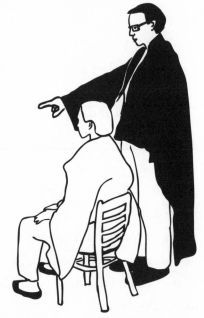

As I looked at Sylvia from across the room, I immediately heard the Editor's response inside my head. I asked the tallest man in the room to play the Editor and draped black around his shoulders. I placed him at Sylvia's elbow, where he pointed a finger at her and said, in a contemptuous voice, "You always get it wrong!"

As I looked at the Sylvia seated at the desk and the Editor pointing at her, I knew there was another player in the scene. It stood off to one side and spoke words of encouragement to Sylvia in a gentle voice. I chose a woman named Charlene to play this encouraging part and draped her in dark brown. After looking at her for a minute, I realized with a shock that she was chocolate! I had somehow enthroned chocolate as a source of support. No wonder I liked brownies so much!

I grasped also that Sylvia should be saying something slightly different. She was the one who wanted to create, but she was also the one who wanted to belong in a group. She wanted to connect both with her creativity and with a group of friends. She was really saying, "I want to connect."

When it was time to decide what I wanted to do with this scene, I wasn't sure at first. I could do what I had done with the bully and shout the Editor down. I had the impression, though, that shouting at it would not really finish the Editor off. Every time I had left a group of women, I could still hear the Editor slicing and dicing me inside my head.

I could do what Lyle had done and ask for a blessing for the writer at the desk. Maybe she could get a blessing from chocolate! That was certainly a creative solution, and since what I wanted was to be creative, that appealed to me. But somehow the idea didn't have much juice in it.

The facilitators offered another option as well: to view this whole scene as something I was carrying, inside me and in my behavior, as a way of loving somebody. I heard their words but I was too distracted to really grasp them. My eyes were fixed on the Editor. It was the real problem. I somehow had to tackle the Editor, or it would stay there, at my elbow, tearing my work apart.

WHO'S GOT THE POWER?

As I thought about what to do next, one of the facilitators asked me, "Who has the power in this scene?"

There was no question about it: the Editor had all the power. It had the power to keep me from writing, to keep me frozen, to keep me out of groups. The writer at the desk wanted to write poetry and stories and plays. She wanted to connect with the creative life force inside her. She also wanted to connect with groups of other women. But the Editor would never let that happen. It was the one calling all the shots.

In a way, the Editor was holding prisoner all the power that I wanted for being creative. Trapped inside my Shaming-Fleeing box was my nine-year-old self wanting to connect. A nine-year-old girl normally has no difficulty connecting. It was only this box that was preventing her from getting what she wanted. Was there a way to liberate that power and bring it to the writer at the desk so she could connect once again?

Yes, there was, but it was the scariest of the options they were offering me. The way to free the prisoner was to play the Editor and become the bad guy. In this supportive place, where there were invisible arms to hold me and skilled facilitators to keep me safe, I could become one of the walls of the box. I would feel what it was like to be a bad guy who had all the power.

The truth was that I already *felt* like the bad guy all the time. I was already acting like the Editor, to myself and others, unintentionally. This was a chance to act like the Editor on purpose in a symbolic way so I could stop doing it by accident. That was the way to fully own my Editor and bring the creative power trapped in it out of prison to use in my life.

Inside the bad guy, there was creative power that was good. The Editor's voice was my father's, and my father certainly had good in him. People had good inside them even if they abused power as my Editor did. And power wasn't all bad either. I needed power to do everything I did during the day, starting with getting out of bed in the morning.

My power for connecting was somehow imprisoned in the Editor's wall of the box. The only way to get it back was to become the wall and feel what power was like.

To play the Editor, I would step into its place standing at Sylvia's elbow. I would wear the black fabric over my shoulders and, with contempt in my voice, say to the writer at the desk, "You always get it wrong!"

Sylvia would step to one side and the writer at the desk would be played by a small, muslin doll stuffed with cotton. The doll would lie on the chair where Sylvia had been sitting, and Sylvie would stand to one side and say, "I want to connect." As the Editor, I would aim my abuse at the doll, just as the Editor had aimed its abuse at me for so many years. I could abuse a cloth doll in any way I chose without doing any harm to Sylvia.

As the facilitators described the process to me, playing the Editor would feel like climbing onto the back of a horse that's already galloping. My job was to let the horse gallop and trample the doll beneath my hooves. I had learned to use the power of this magnificent beast as criticism instead of as power I could use for connecting. Criticism had been trampling me and my friends for years. It was time to do on purpose what I had been doing for years without wanting to. The horse would eventually exhaust itself, and when that happened, I could grab the reins and make the horse go where *I* wanted it to go. I couldn't quite picture what the facilitators were saying, but I knew I wanted to try it. In fact, I was *hungry* to try it. Horses had always scared me, but I had an inkling that I might just find this fun.

There was power in the Editor's contempt, in its merciless attacks on my work, in its criticism of me and my friends. I wanted to use that power for a different purpose, to fuel a life of creativity, to infuse my writing with creative intensity, and to belong in a group of women. This was my chance to get it.

Chapter 11

Enter the Risk Manager

I stood there, looking down at the cloth doll. I knew I needed to start speaking, but something was holding me back. My mouth was dry. I didn't know it yet, but a risk was emerging, a risk so big that it would not even let me speak.

What was at risk for me, the facilitators asked, to really own this Editor in myself?

The answer I heard inside was, *I don't know.* But I couldn't get my mouth to say it.

Was there a part of me, they asked, that found it hard to trust that this process would work for me?

My gut said yes, and I nodded my head. Normally I would have felt guilty about admitting that I didn't completely trust what was happening. That would be like saying I didn't trust the facilitators, who were my friends. To my surprise, I felt relieved to admit it to myself, and to them.

They asked me to choose someone to play the part of me that

found it hard to trust, so it could be present and take part in the process. I asked a woman named Dorothy, and she walked over to stand next to me.

The facilitators asked if they could talk to this part of me directly. I nodded, and I switched places with Dorothy. I handed her the black fabric, and she swung it over her shoulders. She took the Editor's place by the chair and pointed her finger down at the cloth doll. I moved to where she had been standing, assuming the role of the part of me that found it hard to trust, and then turned to face the facilitators.

HONORING MY RISK MANAGER

"Hi!" they said. "So you're the part of Alyce that finds it hard to trust that this process will work for her, is that right?"

I nodded. *This is novel,* I thought to myself, *playing not Alyce but a part of Alyce.* It was kind of exciting.

"Welcome!" they went on, sounding as if they meant it. They said they saw me as a part of Alyce that had been watching out for her for a long time and saving her from doing things that were too risky.

Inside, I felt a huge relief.

"Yes," I said. I was finally speaking.

They said I had probably saved Alyce from many risky situations in her life. They said I might even have saved her life.

Tears came to my eyes. I knew in my heart that there had indeed been times when my life had been in danger, and I was the part that had saved the day. It felt really good to be acknowledged for that.

They said they were really glad that Alyce had a part like me, watching out for her and protecting her from harm. They said they wanted to consult with me about what was happening, because they wanted Alyce to be really safe while she reclaimed her creative life. They said they figured I knew Alyce better than they ever could, and they wanted my advice on how to keep her safe. They called me "a wise voice" inside of Alyce that could advise her on how to stay safe.

No one had ever called me wise before. I had never dared think that any part of me might be considered wise.

They said they often called a part like me a Risk Manager, though I might have a different name for myself. I liked the word "Manager," it had an authoritative sound. I had rarely felt authoritative about anything. They asked me what was at risk for Alyce to own that she had an Editor inside and get her creative writer's life.

I told them about Dad and the way he had criticized Alyce and her siblings. I told them Alyce had felt so stung by his criticism that she had decided at an early age never, *ever* to be like him. The risk in admitting she had an Editor inside was that she might believe she was evil inside and had no way to control the evil. If she had believed that, she would have been unable to trust anything about herself, anything she thought or said or did, because it might be evil.

When I finished, they said that from what they knew of my background, it made sense that it would be very risky for Alyce to admit she had an Editor inside. They said they were glad I had been there all these years to protect Alyce from taking a risk like that. My eyes filled with tears again.

CONTRACTING

They asked me whether there was anything they needed to do to make it safer for Alyce to get her creative life today.

"No," I said immediately. They had listened to me and honored and thanked me for protecting Alyce. I felt completely safe about continuing.

They said that if another risk came up, they would want to ask me about it directly. They asked if I would be willing to stay present in the room and keep an eye out for risks. That way, if they needed to talk to me directly, they could do so. I agreed. They promised to check in with me at the end of the process to make sure everything had gone okay. I had never felt so much in charge before.

They asked if there was anything I, as Risk Manager, wanted to say directly to Alyce before they switched me back into her. I nodded. I turned toward Dorothy, who was still playing me in my role as the Editor.

"I know how much you want the life of a creative writer," I said. "You've wanted it for years. And I want you to go for it. You deserve it."

Then I switched places with Dorothy again. She handed me back the black fabric, and I put it on, resuming the role of Editor.

Dorothy repeated the words I had just said. She said she knew how much I wanted the life of a creative writer and wanted me to go for it. She told me I deserved it.

Tears came to my eyes again. I had a new ally.

The facilitators asked if there was a color for my Risk Manager. It was yellow, I said. As they gave Dorothy a yellow piece of fabric to put around her shoulders, I thought that it made sense, since yellow is the color for caution.

WORKING THE RISK

Wrapped in black, I looked down once again at the cloth doll on the chair.

The facilitators said they had just been talking with my Risk Manager, who considered this process safe enough for me to proceed.

They recapped what the Risk Manager had said. Then they said they believed it was my decision, as Alyce, whether or not to proceed. Now that I was playing Alyce again, they wanted to be sure I was the one making the final choice.

I said yes, I wanted to proceed.

Lastly, now they knew I felt safe enough to proceed, they wanted to ask me about a risk my Risk Manager had mentioned: the risk of believing I had evil inside and feeling I couldn't trust anything about myself because it might be evil.

It was definitely a risk. I had arranged a life for myself that did not include the creativity I longed for, in order to avoid the risk of believing I had evil inside and feeling I couldn't trust anything about myself.

That certainly made sense. I had distrusted myself in groups for years and thought of myself as a bad person, and I knew how painful that was. But once again, I faced an unpleasant truth: I already trusted nothing about myself. I didn't trust myself to play a game with my daughter or write a poem without doing it wrong. I didn't trust myself to mark up a coworker's English paper without tearing it to shreds. Not having a creative writer's life wasn't keeping me from distrusting myself—I distrusted myself anyway.

Since I was already living the worst case scenario, I decided I might as well take the risk. As one of the facilitators put it, I had already paid for the ticket, and I might as well take the ride.

THE HORSE'S HOOVES

I stared down at the cloth doll on the chair. When I moved, the black fabric around my shoulders rippled slightly.

Slowly, carefully, the facilitators talked me through what would happen, advising me on how to proceed and alerting me to the feelings I might encounter. With each instruction, I felt myself drop to a deeper frequency, closer to the pounding hooves.

Lastly, they said that they believed we all have a part like the Editor inside, and I was doing a piece of work here for everyone in the room. They said that when others in the group became aware of their own Editors, they would slap their thighs to let me know they were with me. The atmosphere in the room quivered with excitement.

As the music rose in volume, I said to the doll in a low growl, "You always get it wrong."

A woman in the group said, "Yeah," softly, and began to slap her thighs.

I looked down at the faceless doll lying on the chair, its legs sprawled carelessly. It was so powerless, so pathetic. I felt only contempt. I was the one in control. I began to taunt the doll, as the Editor had taunted me for years.

"You're pathetic," I said to it scornfully. "You think you can write." I poked the doll with my finger. "But you can't write. Who told you that you were a writer? You're not a writer. You're not anything. You're pathetic."

I circled the chair, withering the doll with my gaze and poking it from time to time. Others in the room began to slap their thighs.

I felt powerful for the first time in my life. The horse was galloping, galloping.

MAKING THE CONNECTION

When the horse stopped running, the doll was in tatters. I had pulled it apart with my bare hands and with my teeth, stabbing and biting it as the Editor had sliced and diced me for years on end. I felt as if I were standing on a windswept prairie. I had no more urge to destroy—no urge to do anything specific. There was no more contempt. It had run its course. I closed my eyes and felt a sensation like wind sweeping through me. But it was only a sensation, not the contempt I had been carrying around for years. It was a sensation, no more.

The facilitators asked what the sensation wanted.

My arms, which had been hanging at my sides, instinctively reached out to encircle the air in front of me.

"To reach out," I answered.

What did it want to get by reaching out that it wanted even more than to reach out?

My arms closed on air, and I wanted to hug myself.

"It wants to connect," I said.

A wave of longing washed over me. My knees bent, and I was kneeling on the floor, sobbing, the shiny green fabric held close to my chest. Connection! That was what Dad had wanted when he criticized. He had wanted to connect and had never known how. He had never known any other way to connect with his children or his friends, or with himself, but by criticizing. His own father had suffered the same inability to connect and had drowned his loneliness in alcohol.

I felt so full of love, as if my entire chest cavity were filled with it. There was a river of love inside me that wanted to spill out and flow to everyone and everything I loved.

When I asked the river what it said about me, it said, "I connect."

THE CONSCIOUS PREDATOR

"What was *that*?"

It was Dorothy asking, once the group had reassembled after a break. Dorothy had had a ringside seat for the feeding frenzy as I, in the role of my Editor, had demolished the little muslin doll. During the workshop's first evening, in which the facilitators had described all the shadows, she had heard them refer to one shadow that was darker than all the others, the one known as "the predator." The Editor was clearly just such a predator, and now that she had seen the process that transformed it, she wasn't sure what to make of it.

From the discussion that followed, I understood how controversial this process of tearing apart a muslin doll might be for some people. One woman, who said she had been raised Catholic, exclaimed that if her childhood priest had witnessed my doll-tearing frenzy, he would likely say I had been possessed by the devil.

Having lived with the Editor inside me all these years, I could certainly agree that the Editor was devil-like, but it was clearly a part of me and not something that existed only outside of me. What's more, it was essential that I admit to myself that it *was* a part of me before I could take a close look at it and do something about it.

The facilitators reiterated something they had touched on with me earlier, that it was vital that the predator process be done in symbolic space like this workshop, under the careful guidance and eldership of fully trained and certified facilitators who had done the process themselves.

A man named Gareth said that, when I had first put the black fabric around my shoulders, he'd wondered if it was really okay to act out cruelty so openly. But then, when he saw me discover the river of love trapped inside the predator, he became convinced that he was watching a deeply spiritual transformation, and that keeping the cruelty hidden inside could do much more harm.

"It's natural for us to fear this part of ourselves," he said thoughtfully, "because we so often see it doing evil in the world. But the fact that we fear it only shows what merciful, compassionate people we are, that we don't want anyone to get hurt by it."

There were others in the group who had experienced stepping into their inner predators. A man named Mike said he heard about predators preying on people on the news every day and wished more of them were conscious of the desires lying beneath their behavior.

"I think your dad was just trying to connect," said another man, looking at me. "My dad was the same way. I think many men of his generation had no idea how to relate to their kids."

A man named Ted, who was a chiropractor, said that when he had seen the Editor pointing the finger, he realized it must be his own predator who diagnosed his patients.

"I think it's my predator eyes that look at my patient's spine and spot the vertebrae that are out of alignment," he said. He reached out to touch the spine of his wife, Judy, who was sitting next to him, and she sat up quickly. Everyone laughed.

"And I don't do it to be cruel," he continued. "I do it because my patient wants my help with a problem. Don't you, dear?" He grinned at her.

"Of course, dear," she grinned back. "Just like I want to help *you!*" Her index finger burrowed into his ribs, and they wrestled, laughing. He growled at her playfully. They clasped hands and Judy lay her head on his shoulder, looking happy.

CHANGE IN DIRECTION

During the days and weeks that followed the workshop, I realized that playing the Editor had made a powerful impact on me. I had stepped through my Magician portal and found I no longer distrusted myself. I read, I studied, I talked to the people I met. I began to trust myself as someone who could talk freely without hurting anybody. As I shamed myself less, I aimed less shame at others. I learned to trust my intuition and think on my feet.

I felt an almost insatiable hunger for learning. I began to trust in the process of learning, which would involve making some mistakes. My Magician self learned to use the power of my creative voice to connect with my reader and evoke emotion. I was more in control of my creative process, too, and could seek out inspiration instead of passively waiting for it to strike. I felt much less fear about the future and more trust in life.

I found I had much more stamina for anything I put my mind to. I became a supervisor at work and saw more clearly where I was headed: toward a career as a facilitator.

The wind had picked up, and my sailboat was underway.

Over the next few months, I stepped into the Editor several more times, each time relishing the rhythmic pounding of the horse's hooves and the river of connection they brought me to. Each time I reached the river's edge, the channel had deepened and intensified the flow of connection back into my life.

ONE KITTEN TO GO

My power to connect had been imprisoned inside the Editor. I had learned to use my power in this way from my father, who had in turn learned it from someone else.

The only question that remained was why I had learned to connect through cruelty from Dad, when I might have learned to connect through kindness from someone else. In the answer to this question, an even greater gift awaited me than my power to create, the gift of a new identity.

Chapter 12

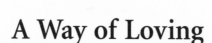

A Way of Loving

At the age of seven, my daughter attended a children's clay class at our local recreation center. She enjoyed it so much that for the next six years she took pottery classes every chance she got. Once, as I was driving her home from class, she told me, "Mom, I love it so much, I don't ever want to stop."

She loved throwing pots and became very adept for her age at centering them on the wheel. What she didn't enjoy was painting them. She told me she had ruined good pots by messing up when she applied the paint.

I struggled to think of what to say, my mind having gone oddly blank.

"I'll bet everybody has trouble with the painting," I said.

I was smiling but didn't feel much of an emotional reaction. She showed me the pots made by her friends, who did seem to apply the paint a little more evenly. I assured her that her pots were beautiful, even as I silently noted their imperfections. I told her I would love her creations no matter what they looked like.

After a few conversations like this, she no longer brought up the subject of painting. When I praised her work, she gave me a wan smile and looked away. I told myself it was natural for her to discount my compliments because I was her mother.

By the time she was twelve, she was proficient enough at throwing to attend adult classes, but I couldn't find a teacher who was willing to take even a well-behaved child into the class. Consequently, I found a potter at a studio on the north side of Chicago who was willing to give private lessons. It was a bit of an ordeal getting down to the city from the suburbs, but I was committed to doing whatever it took to further her art, and I was proud of myself for doing so.

So, after a few months, it was a shock when my daughter announced that she no longer wanted to do ceramics.

"But you're an artist!" I blurted out.

She looked surprised by my outburst but didn't want to talk about it further. As she walked away, I felt a wave of grief welling up inside me, and tears filled my eyes. The intensity of my reaction surprised me. Certainly I had felt pleased and proud that she was creative. I had taken her with me to art museums from the time she was quite young and had imagined the day when I could say to friends with pride, "My daughter is a ceramic artist." Obviously I had an emotional investment in her being artistic.

At this point in my own development, I had taken the advanced facilitation training and could work through many issues on my own. I recognized this wave of grief as a sign that I had experienced a loss of some kind. I resolved to discover what I had lost and somehow reconnect with it. I looked for a time when I had the house to myself, and it soon arrived.

It was one of those rare warm days at the end of autumn. I sat in my living room with my facilitator's manual on my lap, gazing out at the front yard, which was covered in golden leaves lit by the sun. I realized I had left my water bottle in the car. I walked out the front door to get it and breathed in the nostalgic fragrance of drying leaves.

Three hours later, I walked back into the house, having raked the front yard and spread mulch beneath the shrubs. I looked backwards out the door, feeling exceedingly satisfied with my afternoon's work. Closing the door behind me, I turned and gazed around the darkening room and was shocked to see my facilitator's manual sitting on the sofa.

Hunh! I thought to myself. *I had planned to do that, hadn't I?* Fortunately, I would once again have the house to myself the next day while my husband and daughter attended a father-daughter event.

The next day, as soon as they left, I sat down on the sofa, a cup of tea by my side. I felt antsy for some reason. I started a CD of Native American flute music playing on the stereo, hoping it would help ground me. I had just eaten lunch and felt a bit sleepy. *Maybe I'll just rest a while first,* I thought.

It was several hours later when I awoke as my daughter walked into the room.

I realized there must be some kind of risk for me in this wave of grief. But when I asked myself what was at risk, I heard no answer from inside. I wasn't sure what to think.

Risks had arisen before, of course. To get my voice back, I had faced the risk of getting killed. To receive a blessing and feel lovable as I was, I had faced the risk that the support would go away again, and I would be alone. In each case, the risk had caused a ripple in the process that was quickly calmed by acknowledging the good reasons for the risk's existence and then deciding to take it.

To get my power back from the Editor, I had faced the much bigger risk of believing I had evil inside and feeling I couldn't trust anything about myself. That risk had initially threatened to keep me from speaking, which would have effectively stopped the process. Not until the facilitators talked to my Risk Manager directly, and offered reassurance that there had been very good reason for caution, had my Risk Manager given the okay to proceed.

Clearly there was some very big risk here, and so far my Risk Manager was not okay with my proceeding. I knew that I could have a conversation with my Risk Manager about it and try to find out what the risk was. I had done that before with good results. I decided to wait for some quiet time to do that. I was scheduled to leave on a short trip the following day, and I most likely would not have a chance to do it before I left.

SECOND WAVE

My trip was to Wisconsin, to visit family there. Late that afternoon, I found myself in a group of female relatives, all of whom had also experienced Shadow Work. We were drinking tea and try as I might, I couldn't figure out how to enter the conversation. I suddenly felt the old familiar feeling of being an outsider. I finally blurted something out that sounded so ridiculous to my ears, I excused myself and went into the bathroom.

Standing at the sink, I looked at myself in the mirror. A wave of grief welled up inside me and filled my eyes. After all this time, and after all the work I had done, I still felt like an outsider in a group of women, even women with whom I had so much in common. What was wrong with me?

There was a pain in my chest, very much like the loneliness I had hugged to myself as a child. I realized I must still be hugging something to myself that was causing me this pain. But what was it?

An image came back to me of the Editor draped in black, standing beside a writer and pointing at her work with contempt. What had not appeared in my inner play that day was the reaction of the writer at the desk when the Editor attacked her work. I pictured her reaction lying on the floor at her side, a young girl prostrate with grief. The tears filling my eyes as I looked in the bathroom mirror were the girl's tears. The Editor had ridiculed a comment I had made over tea, and I had fled from the room feeling shame and grief, just as I had fled from groups so many times in the past.

TWO PALETTES

When I got home from Wisconsin, I promptly got sick with a mild flu. I saw my illness as just another ploy by my Risk Manager to keep me from examining the issue further. Since I was home from work anyway, I decided to see if I could get to the bottom of it.

I opened my journal and wrote the words, "I want to let go." My eyes filled with tears. I wanted to let go of this painful pattern of feeling that I didn't belong in a group of women. I was pretty sure I *did* belong with the women in Wisconsin, since we had not only family ties but Shadow Work in common, but there was something stopping me from *feeling* I belonged.

I wanted to see the young girl who lay on the floor at the writer's side, prostrate with grief. I pictured her bent over, sobbing, reaching out her arms for something she couldn't have. I grabbed a pillow from the sofa and placed it on the floor. She seemed to be wearing light blue, so I covered the pillow with a light blue piece of fabric.

What was she saying, I asked myself?

"I can't let go, and it's breaking my heart."

I wrote the words on a piece of paper and set it on the floor next to the pillow, feeling that I had never written truer words in my life.

What couldn't she let go of? The feeling that she didn't belong. I pictured myself sitting in a group, belonging but telling myself that I didn't. I brought a large stuffed bear from my daughter's room and placed it a few feet in front of the pillow. Its color seemed to be a rainbow. I wrapped a piece of rainbow-striped fabric around the bear's shoulders.

How was belonging in a group like a rainbow, I wondered? Because with women friends, I wanted to show all of myself, even the critical part of me. I wanted to know that if I said something critical by mistake, I could apologize and still belong, instead of shaming myself and fleeing. As I stood back to survey the scene, the bear's rainbow cloak reminded me of an artist's palette of many colors. As the artist of my own life, I wanted to use all the colors on my palette, even if some of them involved making mistakes. I remembered that I also wanted to let go of my daughter being an artist. It was her choice what to do with her life, not mine. If she didn't want to take ceramics classes any more, that was her business. Somehow, the feeling that I didn't belong in a group and my daughter being an artist were connected, though I didn't know how.

An artist can make mistakes, too; she can start over again with a fresh canvas. The rainbow bear was the Artist: my daughter the artist painting colorful clay pots, and myself as a girl revealing all of herself in a group. The Artist was saying, "I can mess up, and it will be okay."

MAKING A MESS

As I looked at the Artist, it occurred to me that an artist needs something to draw on. I got a piece of blank paper and some colored markers and placed them in front of the bear. The colors looked bright and cheerful in a room suddenly drab by comparison. They seemed to call to me. I wondered what it would be like to play the Artist.

I took the rainbow fabric off the bear and draped it around my own shoulders, moving the bear to one side. I sat down on the floor where the bear had been and took a green marker in one hand. I scribbled on the paper and felt laughter bubbling up from inside me. I laughed out loud and scribbled harder, until the paper was a mess of colored streaks.

On impulse, I crumpled the paper into a ball and threw it across the room. How fun, to make a mess and throw it away! I did it again. I scribbled all over a piece of paper, crumpled it into a ball, and threw it across the room. I burst out laughing, feeling more free than I had felt in a long time. I wanted more colors, so I brought more markers and scribbled with many different colors. I went on laughing as I crumpled up each new piece of paper and threw it across the room.

When the novelty began to wear off, I knew I was done playing the Artist. I wrapped the rainbow fabric around the bear's shoulders again and placed the Artist in its original position on the floor.

The room had changed. There were crumpled pieces of paper everywhere. I walked to the other end of the room and sat on a chair to have a look at it. The Artist had indeed made a mess—of each piece of paper and of the room as a whole.

I looked back at the Artist and suddenly felt a kind of contempt. Sure, it liked making a mess. It didn't have to clean it up! And what was the result of all this mess? Nothing lasting, nothing productive— nothing but mistakes!

It was the second time the word "mistakes" had gone by, and this time it caught my attention. It was a word I had heard all too often from the Editor. I grabbed a piece of black fabric and draped it over the chair where I had been sitting. There was never any question what color the Editor was.

Neither was there much question about what it was saying.

"You think you're an artist?" the Editor sneered. "What a joke. All you do is make mistakes!"

A LONG-FORGOTTEN STORY

The scene seemed complete. All I had to do now was figure out where it had come from. Was there something familiar about this scene? Had I been born with this pattern going on inside me or had I learned it somewhere along the way? Who *were* these people?

There was no question about where I had seen the Editor before. It was Dad. The Artist was me wanting to bring my whole self into a group of friends and still belong. When the Editor was Dad and the Artist was me, who was the blue-covered pillow, lying on the floor, prostrate with grief? It was obviously me, grieving something I had lost.

A memory came to me. I was lying on my stomach on a living room rug, drawing . . .

Chapter 13

Paradise Lost

When I was growing up, Christmas was my favorite time of year, and not just because of the gifts under the tree. It was Dad's favorite time of year, too, and his cloud of trauma seemed to lift a little. He was less irritable, less taciturn, and he even spent time with his children, which almost never happened at other times of year. I don't know how old I was when I realized that he was keeping us out of the house while Mom wrapped gifts, but it still meant a great deal to me.

One of my most vivid Christmastime memories is of Dad taking us on a tramp through newly fallen snow. We were bundled until we could barely move, in snow pants and parkas, skating socks, black rubber boots with black metal buckles, mittens and mufflers, hats and hoods. Dad wore a hat with turn-down ears, and his ruddy complexion turned bright red in the cold air.

He led us to the end of our street and along the path that led to our church, where the buildings stood black and silent. There, in a small grove of evergreens, Dad gathered us around him and grabbed a fir tree weighted down with branch loads of soft snow. His hands, in brown work gloves, shook the trunk. An avalanche slithered past our faces, over our shoulders and down our boot-tops, while we bent our heads and closed our eyes. When the avalanche finished, we came alive and shook and giggled. Dad laughed to see us coated in snow, and we laughed back. I knew he was laughing at our expense, but he was my Dad, and we had him all to ourselves, and it was Christmastime.

Considering the tight budget Mom and Dad held to for the rest of the year, we each received an impressive abundance of Christmas gifts. It was risky, however, to ask for anything in particular because it might not be possible. Mom's usual response to a special request was, "I'll take it up with the War Department."

The Christmas I was nine, I took the risk. Somewhere I had seen an advertisement for Venus Paradise Coloring Pencils, and I had never seen anything so beautiful in all my life. The smooth, round, slender pencils, each engraved with the name of its color, were so much more elegant and grown-up than crayons. I was sure I would color expertly with them, without those annoying smears of wax that crayons left on the paper. And the colors were so vibrant. I wanted to draw pictures that blazed with color.

I remember inspecting my pile of gifts that Christmas morning and spotting the one that was about the right size and shape. Could it be, could it really be? As I saw the words "Venus Paradise" emerge from the wrapping paper, I cried out with joy.

In the days that followed, I drew picture after picture with my beloved pencils. I tried tracing a few famous paintings from pages in our encyclopedia, but they proved too difficult to duplicate. I could do rainbows, though, in a myriad variations.

It was late one afternoon that I was lying on my stomach on the living room rug, drawing happily on a piece of paper that rested on the smooth surface of a large, hardcover book of nursery rhymes. My picture was a design using my favorite colors, including my most favorite of all, emerald green. I had seen a picture of an emerald once in a library book about gems and had stared for a long time into its mysterious depths. Green was Dad's favorite color, and pastel green paint covered the walls of the room.

Dad came into the room and sat in an armchair nearby. I glanced up at him and saw on his face that he was tense and irritable. Mom was seated in the next room at the dining room table, writing letters and paying bills. Dad told Mom he'd just been on the phone with George. Dad began ridiculing George, as I had heard him do before.

"You know what he told me?" Dad asked Mom. "That he thinks he's one of the handsomest men in the church." Dad laughed derisively. "What a jackass!"

Mom chided him, nodding in my direction, and went into the kitchen. I had never thought much about George's appearance. *He's not handsome,* I thought to myself, as I reached for the Peacock Blue. *But then, neither is Dad, not really.* I glanced surreptitiously up at him.

"Ugly as a mud fence," Dad said. He threw back his head and laughed loudly.

He looked down at me, and I felt suddenly afraid. My arm instinctively circled my picture. I saw his eyes follow my movements.

"Ugly as a mud fence," he said again, looking at me, his tone a savage smirk. I stared at him, unable to look away. Did he mean George was ugly? Did he mean my drawing? Or . . . did he . . . mean *me?* Was he saying *I* was as ugly as a mud fence? My pulse pounded in my ears. My legs were frozen.

"Another masterpiece you got there?" He looked from me to my picture and back again. He laughed derisively, again throwing his head back.

My face burned, as if I had been dipped in boiling water. I looked down at the floor so that our eyes would not meet again. I stood up, picked up my drawing, went into my room and closed the door. I again heard his laugh from the living room.

I sat on the edge of my bed. When I looked at my drawing, my chest hurt. I opened a drawer in my desk and slipped the drawing in. I curled up on the bed and put my thumb in my mouth. I knew only babies sucked their thumbs and I didn't care.

My world had changed.

BEFORE THE FALL

Before Dad walked into the room, when I was drawing happily, my inner world had been quite animated. My Magician was sensibly planning what my picture would look like and objectively analyzing the result so far. She was saying to herself, "This picture is better than the last one I drew. I'm learning to control the way I use the pencils so the picture comes out the way I planned it. I trust this process, and I trust myself to learn and improve. I'll learn from teachers and artists who know how to draw well, and what they can't teach me, I'll figure out on my own."

My Warrior was feeling strong and wanted to test her strength with a further challenge. "I'm working hard and making it real! I'm getting a solid grounding in technique here, which will serve me well as I progress. I am capable of accomplishing what I set out to do. I am proving myself! I will continue working hard and become the best artist in the whole world!"

My Sovereign was blessing the scene serenely, delighting in the rainbow that blazed from my colored pencils. "This is going well, and I feel good about myself. I love drawing so much, I could do it all day long! If I need any help, I'll ask someone, and they'll support me. I'm so grateful I received these pencils. Their colors fill with me joy. Creating this picture means something, too. I have a vision that art will be my life. I can help other people draw, too."

My Lover was playfully humming a little song. "I love drawing, and I love my colored pencils, and I love my mom and dad for giving them to me. I love bright colors. They make me feel good inside. I draw pretty pictures here, in this warm, cozy house surrounded by these people I love. I belong here, and I'll share this beautiful picture with my family because I want to share with them the pretty pictures that are inside me, and they'll love me the way I love them. I'll always belong here, and we'll always be together."

A TERRIBLE CHOICE

Until my world changed, it would not have occurred to me that there was anything wrong with my lying on the rug, drawing a picture with my beautiful new pencils, and letting Dad see what I was doing. But it certainly seemed that way now.

It's not that I wasn't resilient. If I had been accepted unconditionally and praised for my creative efforts until then, Dad's verbal attack might only have hurt my feelings momentarily. I might have soon forgotten all about it if he had taken me into his arms and apologized—explained that he was hurting that day and that it wasn't about me—and said that he loved me and was proud of me for being creative.

If, on the other hand, Dad's attack meant that, in this family, my inner world—thinking I was doing well, trusting myself to learn and improve, believing I could be the best, feeling good about myself, expecting support when I needed it, finding meaning, envisioning a life of art, believing I could help others, feeling I belonged, expressing myself creatively—was worthy of contempt and derision, then eventually I was going to *get it*, whether it was the first time Dad ridiculed me, or the third time or the seventh time.

When I *got it*, I was faced with a terrible choice. I could retain that inner world, which until moments before had felt natural and right and good. Or I could exchange it for a different inner world, one in which I didn't belong, couldn't express myself creatively, couldn't trust myself, didn't feel good about myself, didn't believe in myself or my ability to help others, expected no support, found no meaning— and one in which I believed that there was something wrong with me for *ever having thought otherwise*.

My choice wasn't a conscious one. I'm sure I wasn't aware of anything except that, after feeling good, I now felt bad. The bad feeling was shame. Shame told me that if Dad looked inside me, he would find something wrong with me and stop loving me.

At that age, I loved the people around me, all the time, with everything I had. I loved them no matter who they were, and no matter what they did to me. They were my world and I was willing to do anything to adapt to them and fit in. I did anything I had to do in order to belong. There was nothing more terrifying to me than the possibility that the people I loved would not love me back.

I had a choice, but there was really no contest. My love for Dad, and my need to be loved by him, made the choice a certain one. I accepted the belief that there was something wrong with feeling that I belonged, and with *me* for believing it. Accepting that belief hurt me, but I really had no choice. It was the only way to go on loving my Dad and being loved by him.

THE REACTIONS WITHIN

As I accepted the belief that there was something wrong with me, I exchanged one inner world for another. The new one came into being as the parts of me responded to the storm of emotions inside me.

I felt afraid, and my Magician responded to the fear.

"Maybe I don't know how to draw at all," my Magician said, suddenly doubting herself. "I must have been fooling myself. Clearly, I can't trust myself to see how I'm really doing. I certainly didn't know how Dad was going to react to my picture, or I would have hidden it from him. I should have known better. I made a big mistake." My Magician started to sound like the Editor.

I felt angry, and my Warrior answered with a challenge.

"I must not have been working hard enough at this," my Warrior said, amping up the challenge. "I'll just have to work harder, that's all. Just wait and see, I'll *prove* I can do it! This will be my top priority. I won't waste a second of my time on anything frivolous." My Warrior started to sound like the bullying athletic coach.

I felt resigned, and my Sovereign sighed. My Sovereign's usual job was to respond to joy, and it recognized resignation as joy in dull clothing.

"He's my father, and he must be right," my Sovereign sighed, resolved to accept what she must. "This must not be going well after all. Believing that was too good to be true. I don't deserve to do what I love. I'm not good enough to be an artist. If I'm no good at this, I certainly can't help anyone else draw either." The wind had gone out of my sails. My Sovereign started to sound like the becalmed sailor.

More than any other feeling, though, I felt grief—because I had lost something precious. My Lover responded with what comfort it could offer.

"I must not be loving Dad right," my Lover said sadly. "A daughter who loved her father right wouldn't mind if he ridiculed her picture. To love Dad, I've got to take his ridicule and hug it to my chest because that's my bond with him. Yes, it's painful, but if pain is what it takes to love him, then at least I'll be loving him, and I'll be a loving daughter. I've got to hold this pain to my chest and never let it go." My Lover started to sound like a child sitting in a puddle, crying and unable to let go.

There was a payoff of sorts in taking on this painful bond. I would never again be completely alone, for I had something to hug to my chest at night. I couldn't hug my father to my chest, but I could hug this painful new way of loving him. If that's what it took to love my dad, then that's what I would do.

TAKING AN IDENTITY

When I hugged the pain to my chest, a name appeared on the prow of the sailor's boat: *I Don't Connect.* Whenever I felt frustrated about not having a creative life, the sailor even offered me a cover story for *I Don't Connect,* in the form of an identity that helped explain it. I was above being superficial, and the name on the prow became *The Intellectual.* I preferred to spend time by myself, and the name on the prow became *The Loner.* I climbed trees and played baseball and didn't find girls fun to play with anyway, and the name on the prow became *The Tomboy.*

Each of the identities helped me feel a little better about not connecting and each, in its way, provided a convenient defense against connecting at all.

Chapter 14

Choosing a Strategy

Accepting the belief that there was something wrong with me gave me something to hug to my chest at night when I felt alone. But it also left me with a dilemma. What should I do the next time I felt like lying in the middle of the living room rug and drawing a picture, so that I wouldn't get hurt like this again? I needed advice about how to *go on*.

Advice arrived, compliments of my Magician. Whenever I felt afraid, my inborn abilities to learn, to assess risks and to develop strategies for minimizing them came through my Magician portal. Now I certainly felt afraid at the prospect of ever getting ridiculed by Dad again. My Magician's job was to help me understand the risks involved in drawing and learn strategies for staying safe in my new inner world. She offered me three strategies from which to choose.

Strategy number one was to act as I had already acted: to draw a picture when I felt like it, as if nothing were wrong. But now that was very difficult to do. I had been hurt by Dad's ridicule, so I associated drawing with being hurt and ridiculed.

I also had a lot of strong emotions about what had happened. I felt sad that I couldn't simply enjoy drawing pictures any more. I felt angry at Dad for ridiculing me. I felt afraid that he might be right about me, that my picture might be as ugly as a mud fence, that *I* might be as ugly as a mud fence. I felt resigned to living in a family where creative expression wasn't safe. These feelings would undoubtedly surface if the same thing happened again, and they would do nothing to help me bond with Dad. On the contrary, they would tend to create further conflict with him. For a nine-year-old girl who had not yet learned how to hide her feelings effectively, it was simply too risky to let those feelings surface. Strategy number one was out of the question.

Strategy number two required that I put away my beloved colored pencils and never draw pictures again, or at least never allow Dad to see me doing it. This "Never Again" strategy was based on the assumption that if I never let Dad see another one of my pictures, Dad would not find something wrong with me, and he would not stop loving me.

Strategy number three took the opposite approach. It required that I draw constantly until Dad relented, essentially battering on Dad's door until he couldn't stand the pounding any more and stopped ridiculing me. This "In-Your-Face" strategy was based on the assumption that if I kept at it and never gave up, Dad would decide there wasn't anything wrong with me, and he would not stop loving me.

Strategies number two and three would each help me keep my tenuous connection with Dad. With the Never Again strategy, I would be bouncing off the walls, pleading, "Why do I have to hide my pictures in a drawer? Why can't I draw when I want to?" With the In-Your-Face strategy, I would still be bouncing off the walls but with a different plea. "Why do I have to keep this up all the time? Why can't I give it a rest?" Regardless of the strategy I chose, I would be trapped in a box and bouncing off the walls, pleading, "Why are these walls still here? Why am I not free to do as I please? *What's wrong with me?*"

Each strategy would also cause conflict: the In-Your-Face strategy would bring me into conflict with others, while the Never Again strategy would cause more conflict inside me. In our home, conflict was avoided at all costs, so it was natural for me to choose the Never Again strategy.

ENDS OF A LOOP

Choosing the Never Again strategy didn't mean, however, that I never drew again. Each strategy was an uncomfortable extreme and like balancing on one foot, it took an enormous amount of energy to maintain. No strategy could override the *wanting* on the part of my nine-year-old self inside the box. My longings to be in a circle of friends and for creative expression were a natural part of me, like waves lapping at the threshold of the Lover portal from the ocean beyond. Every time I encountered someone who exhibited the connection or the creative expression I longed for, the nine-year-old started bouncing off the walls of the box until it rang like an alarm clock.

That's when the risk arose that the nine-year-old would try "thinking outside the box" and get hurt all over again. The real problem with having my nine-year-old self inside a box was not that I couldn't have access to her. The problem was that I had no *control* over her. That's precisely why it felt like a box: I was trapped in a pattern I couldn't consciously stop. On the day I decided not to draw in order to stay connected with Dad, I gave up that control, and the nine-year-old who wanted to draw pretty pictures went to live inside the box.

From my Magician's point of view, the risk of my getting out of the box was enormous. I risked getting ridiculed again, I risked Dad no longer loving me, I risked never again belonging in my family. For a nine-year-old girl, belonging in her family is crucial to her emotional survival, not to mention her physical well-being. In a very real way, when the nine-year-old began bouncing off the walls, my survival was at risk.

Luckily for me, my Magician was on the lookout for risks. With a wave of her wand, my Magician commissioned a Risk Manager to stand guard over the box and keep me inside it. My Risk Manager scanned the horizons for threats, which generally consisted of any situation that resembled the incident with Dad, and reminded me to keep using the Never Again strategy to avoid getting hurt.

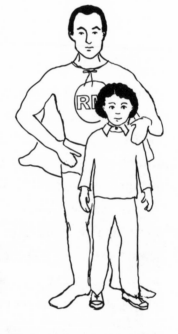

I sometimes ignored my Risk Manager's warnings and tried "thinking outside the box," as when I formed the mom-and-tot group and charged in like an overeager puppy. It felt at first as if I had left the box behind, but that had been an illusion. I had merely flipped from the Never Again strategy into the In-Your-Face strategy. The two strategies were like the two ends of a loop, twin polarities that I alternated between for years. At the center of that loop was the spot where I had been hurt, so I could never stay there for long. I was forced instead to hurtle past it when the anguish of one extreme drove me to the other. The

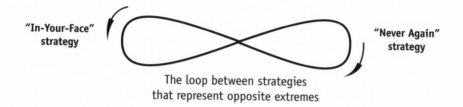

"In-Your-Face" strategy

"Never Again" strategy

The loop between strategies
that represent opposite extremes

Divine sent me many opportunities to experience both sides of the loop so I could learn it well and get the broadest possible range of gifts from the box when I finally learned to transform it.

It's no accident that the loop looks like the symbol for infinity, because that's exactly what it represents: a pattern that would repeat indefinitely in my life until I decided to change it.

Standing squarely in the way of change, however, was my Risk Manager.

Chapter 15

A Memorial to Dad

I stood in my living room, looking at the Artist, a stuffed bear draped in a rainbow. I had forgotten that love of drawing; it seemed so long ago.

One part of me had not forgotten, the blue pillow that lay prostrate on the floor, weeping. I glanced around the room, where my favorite paintings and prints hung on the walls. Now I understood the hunger that had been driving me to museums and galleries all these years with my unwilling daughter in tow. It was this prostrate part of me that had wanted her to share my love of drawing, that wanted her never to give it up.

The Editor had not forgotten my love of drawing either. It sat on the chair, cloaked in black, and maintained its barrage of contemptuous criticism just in case I had any misguided ideas about resuming my artistic career.

Looking at the Editor, I felt fear like a whisper on the back of my neck. A risk was circling the room again; I could feel it. I had forgotten about the risk, but obviously my Risk Manager had not. I knew I should be glad she was reappearing so I could address her, but I wasn't glad. I was afraid.

I stooped to light a candle on the table next to me, then watched its flame flicker and grow bright. Whatever the risk was, I knew it was there for a good reason, and I would find out what it was. I murmured thanks to my Risk Manager for trying to protect me, and I felt her relax a little.

I stepped farther back, hoping I would see why I felt so afraid. I looked back and forth between the Artist and the Editor. *Thank goodness*, I thought to myself, *that I never unleashed my Editor on my daughter's artwork, or she might have stopped creating as I did.*

But wait . . . she had decided to give up ceramics! How could that be? How could I have held back all my Editor's criticism of her painting technique and seen the same result?

My heart was pounding in my chest. There wasn't enough air in the room.

I had been standing in this room when my daughter told me she didn't paint well. My mind had gone oddly blank—my Editor had become clueless! I had felt nothing and said only that her friends probably had the same problem. Instead of connecting with her, I had become stoic! She had wanted to do a better job of painting, and I had done nothing to assist her. I had acted like a passive bystander! She had confided in me about a problem, and I had told her to ignore it. I had told her she could solve the problem by denying it, sounding like the go-getter! I had not protected her from my Shaming-Fleeing box at all—I had merely turned it inside out.

This was the risk my Risk Manager had tried to keep me from seeing during those two earlier attempts to work the issue through, when I had spent one afternoon raking leaves and another afternoon napping.

The risk was seeing that I had done to my daughter exactly what my father had done to me even though I had tried to do just the opposite.

I closed my eyes and covered my face with my hands. I felt so much shame it was almost unbearable. I heard the Editor's voice inside my head telling me I was a terrible parent.

When I opened my eyes, they rested on the candle. My hands moved to my chest, and I remembered the glow there that was gold like the sun. I was lovable the way I was. No, I wasn't a terrible parent at all. I had simply been loving my daughter the same way my Dad had loved me, by passing on a painful pattern.

LOSS OF A LOVED ONE

The scene before me was the final wall of the box that I had been trapped in for so many years.

I had been carrying this box as a way of honoring, and staying connected to, and never forgetting, and memorializing someone I had loved and then lost in a painful way. When I felt the pain of that loss, I had seized a way to keep that loved one with me, as a kind of memorial. Because the loss was painful, I had seized something that was painful to carry—a box—so I would remember the pain of the loss itself.

I had lost two connections that day: one with Dad and one with the little girl who wanted to be an artist. The girl who lay weeping had been feeling the grief of those losses ever since. She was the part of me who had been holding onto the Shaming-Fleeing box as a way of loving.

Knowing that this scene was a memorial told me that I didn't have to carry it any more. I could exchange it for a new way of loving that would work better for me in my life than this Shaming-Fleeing box ever had. To change what happened inside me and act differently from now on, I needed to give this way of loving back to both of them. A box, I realized, has both exterior and interior walls. The four exterior walls faced outwards toward another person, in this case, my dad. The four interior walls faced inwards toward myself, in this case, my artistry.

Was there a word or phrase that summed up this box I had been trapped in? The words "paradise lost" came to me. I had lost the paradise of drawing uninhibitedly and of feeling that I could belong in a group of people who loved me.

MESSAGE OF LOVE

From my bedroom closet, I took a flannel shirt that had belonged to my father and hung it over the back of the Editor's chair. I pictured Dad sitting there, looking back at me.

I searched inside my body for the source of the tears I had been shedding every time I knew I needed to let go. The tears lived in my chest. I pulled the light blue fabric off the pillow, folded it into a small bundle, and clutched it to my chest with one hand. How many times I had felt "blue" over the years as I mourned the groups I left.

I chose some tender music to play on the stereo and knelt beside my father's chair.

"Dad," I said softly, "I've been carrying something for you. I've been carrying the way you ridiculed people so that you wouldn't get close to them. It's kept me from feeling that I belonged in any group of girls or women, for years and years." My voice caught, but I went on.

"That's something I want so badly, Dad—to feel part of a group of women. I'm sure you had your reasons for ridiculing people. Maybe you got ridiculed when you were a boy, I don't know. But it's not working for me to carry this any longer, Dad. I want to have women friends and enjoy their company and feel like one of them. I want to share myself with them and get their support. This pattern is standing in my way. I'm so tired of feeling that I don't belong. I don't want to feel that way any more."

I told him about the four walls of the box: about the girls I had hurt with my ridicule, about how hard I had tried to fit in, about how sad I had felt when I left, and about the labels I had given myself.

"I'll bet you felt like a loner, too, Dad, especially when you returned from the War," I told him. "Most of your friends back home didn't see the kind of combat you did." He had told me once that he never joined an organization for veterans because he thought the men who gathered there were merely congratulating themselves on having survived. I felt sure that Dad suffered from survivor guilt for having outlived his friends and that guilt had made him feel even more like an outsider.

I paused. Had I said everything? No, there was one thing more.

"Dad," I said, picturing his face looking back at me. "I've carried this for you because I loved you." My voice caught again, and I went on. "I loved you so much. I wanted so much for you to love me, and I was never sure you did. I wanted you to be so proud of me; I wanted to be your little girl. I could feel how unhappy you were and I wanted to help you, but I didn't know how."

I still clutched the light blue bundle to my chest. With my other hand, I picked up the end of Dad's flannel sleeve and rested my hand on the chair where his lap would be. I pictured him taking my hand.

"And Dad," I went on, "I realized something just today about this: that I tried to do things differently with my own daughter. I tried to turn off the critical part of me so that I wouldn't criticize her the way you criticized me. But that didn't work either. When I turned off the critical part of me, it became clueless and couldn't advise her. I wanted her to feel good about her creativity, but it turned out just the same.

"I want to find a different way of loving you," I finished, "one that won't keep me from feeling that I belong. I want that so much, Dad, and I just can't live without it any longer."

I pictured my love for him passing through my fingers into the shirt, into his hand. I pictured my message of love going right into his body.

Now it was time to switch places and hear this from the other side.

THE OTHER SIDE

I stood up and laid the bundle of light blue fabric on the floor. I took the flannel shirt off the back of the chair and put it on, then sat down in the chair. I closed my eyes and imagined that I was Dad. I pictured his body, his large chest, large hands, and strong jaw. I sat up straight, molding my body into a more rigid posture. Dad's body had always felt armored, as if there were a layer of metal beneath his skin. I allowed myself to become Dad.

When I opened my eyes again, I pictured Alyce kneeling before the chair, clutching the bundle of light blue fabric to her chest with one hand and holding my large hand with the other. I pictured her talking to me, resting her hand in my lap and sending her love to me through her fingers. She told me about the groups she had belonged to, and about her longing for a group of women friends. She told me that she had done all this as a way of loving me.

Something stirred in my heart. I felt a wave of grief, and my body curled forward with it, until I was doubled over.

"It's not yours," I whispered. "It's mine; it has nothing to do with you." From the depth of my knowledge of the man my father was, came the words to speak. Images flashed through my mind of Dad at social events and family gatherings and work parties for the church, where he turned from others and stood alone or lingered around the edges. He had never been comfortable in groups. I remembered him carving wood in his basement shop, his face lit with satisfaction. I saw him arriving home from his white-collar job, looking empty. He had wanted a creative life, too, and had managed to steal a few moments during the evening in which to indulge his longing.

I pictured myself as Dad looking into Alyce's eyes.

"I've always felt like an outsider who didn't belong," I told her. "I'm so sorry. This isn't yours. It was mine and I never knew what to do about it. I'm so glad that you're learning what to do about it so you don't have to suffer with it the way I did."

I pictured my hand squeezing Alyce's hand in my lap and sending her a message through the touch.

"I did love you, Alyce," I said, "and I'm so sorry that I could never tell you that. I never learned how to tell people what I felt about them, not even my own children. I didn't know how to be a father. I don't think my father knew either. This doesn't belong to you. You learned it from me. And I want you to give it back to me, so you don't have to carry it any more."

I pictured myself squeezing her hand, and I looked into her eyes and sent her my love through Dad's hand and through his eyes. I imagined that I could see it going right into her body. I took a deep breath.

LOVE YOU WILL

Again, I switched places, so that I was once again kneeling on the floor, with the light blue bundle clutched to my chest in one hand and Dad's sleeve in the other, resting where his lap would be. I took a moment to come back into Alyce.

I pictured Dad seated on the chair, clutching my hand. I heard him tell me that the pattern had nothing to do with me. I heard him telling me about his own experiences in groups and how glad he was that I was finding out what to do about it. I heard him say he loved me and didn't want me to carry this for him any more. I felt his love for me come right into my body.

Dad had told me the light blue bundle was his. I gently laid it on his lap and took a deep breath. My chest felt different without that bundle of hurt and loneliness clutched to it.

It was time to speak aloud the words that expressed the belief about what it means to carry something painful for somebody. The words still bring up emotion in my throat although I've spoken them hundreds of times.

> "Love isn't something you do,
> it's something you are.
> You can't stop.
> And if you cannot love joyfully,
> then you will love painfully,
> but love you will,
> because love you are.
>
> "I may have been thinking
> that I didn't love Dad well enough,

>when in fact,
>I was loving him
>with everything I had.
>And anyone who can love
>in that painful way
>has proven her love
>and can love in any way she chooses."

I had been believing all these years that I was too critical to belong. I had been believing that when I said something critical to a girlfriend in a group, it meant I wasn't a loving person. In fact, I had been loving my dad by being critical the way he was, and criticizing my friends in order to belong with *him*. In giving back this pattern to Dad, I was reclaiming my identity as a person who loved *so deeply* that I had been willing to suffer the pain of my Shaming-Fleeing box rather than lose my unconscious bond with Dad. That identity, as a loving person who has proven her love, was one of the gifts inside my Shaming-Fleeing box. If I had never been trapped inside that box, I would not have had such vivid proof of the depth of love of which I was capable.

TAKING GREEN

I wanted another way to stay connected to Dad to replace the pattern I had given back to him. Was there a quality of his that I loved that I would enjoy incorporating into my life?

Yes—his love of nature. Dad's favorite color was green because he loved the outdoors so much. After retiring, he had become a nature photographer. I selected a piece of shiny green lamé fabric and clutched it to my chest, breathing deeply, picturing myself breathing in all the freshness of nature. Feeling that sensation of freshness in my lungs, I asked the freshness, "What do you have to say to me, *about* me?"

"I belong," it replied. I belonged in nature, and in a circle of women friends.

Chapter 16

Memorial to the Artist

I had given back to Dad my painful way of loving him and found another way to belong, by belonging in nature.

Now I wanted to give back to the Artist my painful way of loving her.

I found a shallow box of about the right size to hold the colored markers and arranged them in it so that it looked like a box of colored pencils. *How fitting,* I thought, *to put the markers in a box, since my Artist had been living in a box for all these years.* I selected a dull gray piece of fabric and wrapped the box of markers in it so that it looked like a tombstone. How gray my life had been since I gave up my creative life! On a piece of paper, I wrote, "Here lies my Artist—R.I.P.," and taped it to the fabric.

I searched inside my body for the location of the gray tombstone. It was in my chest, as the blue bundle had been. I clutched the gray tombstone to my chest with one hand.

I knelt beside the Artist, who sat on the rug beside her colored markers. I pictured myself as a girl drawing a picture next to her box of colored pencils. I saw the curly dark hair, the bright blue eyes, the ruddy cheeks, the sensitive, quirky mouth. As a girl, my name had been Alice Ann.

"Alice Ann," I said, "I've been carrying something for you. I've been carrying the way you put your artistry away. I know you had a good reason—because it hurt so much when Dad ridiculed you. But it's not working for me to carry this for you any longer. I want to write creatively again, but I haven't been able to for years and years. I want to connect with the creative force that's inside me and express myself creatively in any way I want, without fear of criticism."

I told her about the poems I had written and torn apart, and about the poems I had smothered at birth because I knew I couldn't finish them, and about the harsh words I had used for my writing: boring, obvious, cliché. I told her that I had stopped even reading poetry because it had become too painful and how much I missed it.

"I carried this for you because I loved you," I told her. I took the bear's hand and held it on my lap, picturing my hand clasping the hand of a little girl.

"You were so creative, so passionate about color. You had so much fun. I know that putting away your creativity and living in a box was the right decision for you, but I can't live that way any more. I don't even want to wear gray clothes any more. I want to wear the bright colors you loved."

I sent my love for her through my hand, into her body. I saw my love going right into her body.

Then it was time to switch places and hear this from the other side.

BEING ALICE ANN

I moved the bear to one side and sat on the floor where it had been, draping its rainbow fabric around my shoulders. I laid the gray tombstone on the floor beside me where I had been kneeling.

I closed my eyes and pictured myself as nine years old again. I pictured my body becoming the limber body of a young girl. I imagined myself running easily about the room, skipping, hopping, doing somersaults. I allowed myself to become Alice Ann, the child.

When I opened my eyes again, I pictured Alyce, the adult, kneeling before me. She clutched the gray tombstone to her chest with one hand and held my young hand with the other. She talked with a tenderness as one talks to a child, holding my hand, sending her love to me through the touch.

"Alice Ann," I heard Alyce the adult saying, "I've been carrying something for you." She told me about the poems she loved to write and her longing to write creatively again. She told me that she had put away her artistry as a way of loving me and didn't want to do that any more.

From the liveliness in my body that felt like a young girl came the words to speak.

"I don't want you to carry that any more," I told her, looking at the gray tombstone she clutched to her chest. "I decided not to draw any more because it didn't feel safe, but you don't have to make that decision for me any more. I want you to be happy and draw and write poems and create as much as you want to."

I squeezed her hand and sent my love to her through my fingers.

"I love you, too," I said, "and I'm happy that I'm going to grow up to be someone like you who cares this much about being creative. You can throw that away," I said, nodding toward the tombstone.

"You don't need to carry it any more. Go on, and live a creative life. I know you can do it, I have faith in you."

I beamed at her with my eyes, sending her my love, and I saw it go right into her body.

LOVING WITHIN AND WITHOUT

Again, we switched places, so that I was once again kneeling on the floor beside the bear, with the gray tombstone clutched to my chest in one hand and the Artist's hand in the other. I took a moment to come back into Alyce.

I heard the Artist repeating the words I had just spoken. "I don't want you to carry that any more." I heard her love for me, and her faith in me, and I felt it come into me through the touch. I felt her love for me come right into my body.

I unwrapped the box of markers. Using both hands, I wadded up the gray fabric into a ball and threw it as hard as I could across the room. I took a deep breath. My chest felt very different without that tombstone clutched to it.

I had been believing all these years that I didn't love the Artist inside me because I wasn't writing creatively. In fact, I had been loving her with everything I had, by squashing my creative efforts just as she had. I had loved her so deeply that I had been willing to suffer the pain of poems smothered at birth rather than sever my connection with her.

A LOVE OF COLOR

Was there something I wanted to take from the Artist as a way of remembering her and keeping my connection with her?

Yes—her love of bright colors. I wanted to bring that love of bright colors into my closet and use it to transform my wardrobe from gray into all the colors of the rainbow.

I wrapped the rainbow fabric once more around my shoulders, clasping the ends of the fabric with both hands over my chest. I took a deep breath, as if I were breathing all the colors in the fabric right into my chest. When my chest felt full, I asked the colors, "What do you have to say to me, about me?"

"I am connected," the rainbow answered. I was connected with all the colors inside myself and with the creative force inside me that would use those colors to brighten and bring joy to my life.

When I had entered the living room to get to the bottom of the pattern, I had wanted to feel connected. I had new sensations in my chest that said, *I belong* and *I'm connected.*

I was done. I had let go and could finally move on from my Shaming-Fleeing box.

When I discovered how loving I had been all along, I found my Lover portal to connection of all kinds: with my creative force, with other women, with my daughter, with everyone and everything. Giving back this painful pattern to Dad had opened the doorway to my Lover self who could feel deeply, create, be sensual, be luscious, be colorful and have fun. The girl crying in a puddle was now diving and splashing in a pool. I felt lighter than I had in years, as if I had unloaded a heavy burden.

GIFTS IN THE BOX

I saw dramatic changes in my life from taking these new ways of loving my father and my Artist. Those changes are among my favorite aspects of my life today.

The most immediate change was that my writing really took off.

At times I felt like a woman going through labor, waking up at all times of the night with ideas that demanded to be written down. Occasionally an idea arrived as a fully-formed essay that I only had to write down. I told a friend that I had come so far from having writer's block that I was finding it hard to shut up! After a while, I was relieved when what had begun as a deluge of creative ideas calmed down to a reliable stream.

I also looked for an outlet as a visual artist and found great pleasure and satisfaction in designing websites. I realized just recently that I have also learned to "paint" complex concepts by describing them in simple images, such as the image of the box in this book.

A more gradual change was the impact of "taking green" from Dad. I had not been much of an outdoors person since childhood, when I had loved climbing trees in the woods near our house. I now began spending free time in forests, walking or sitting beside streams and playing at dam-making with mud and stones. Even seeing rivulets of water running down the sides of the street fills me with joy. I now live in Colorado and hike in the Rockies.

Most meaningfully, nature has become a vital source of inspiration and solace. It is the church I attend. I communicate with the Divine by watching nature's signals and learning what animals and birds symbolize. Animal medicine is now a fun and richly fulfilling facet of my spirituality. I live my life by the cycles of nature by honoring the seasons and the phases of the moon and the solar year.

I have the creative life I always wanted. I write a lot and am told I write pretty well. I have also created a network of women friends and family members to whom I can show my true colors. I belong to numerous groups that give my life a freshness and a color it never had before. One of them is a large group of women in media that used to meet only for morning coffee once a week and a potluck supper once a month. I preferred late afternoon to morning, so I started a weekly drop-in happy hour called the Schmooze, and at this writing, it's been active for more than three years. Once a month I sing shape note music with a group in Boulder, and I attend networking events several times a month with a local small business organization. Once a year I gather with Shadow Work colleagues and am sometimes the one who starts the puppy pile.

MY INNER CRITIC

Another gift I took from working with my Shaming-Fleeing box was my Editor, whom I have renamed my Inner Critic, a term borrowed from Voice Dialogue created by Hal and Sidra Stone. What my Critic really wanted all along was to help me improve, by pointing out what I was doing wrong so that I could learn to do better. It went about it in a painful way, by shaming me, but its motives were good: it wanted to help me become the best person I could be.

I've learned to use my Critic in a very different way than when I used it to shame myself and to criticize my women friends. I've learned to use it to heal, not to hurt. It was my Critic who helped me learn how to facilitate Shadow Work by pointing out to me the mistakes I made along the way. It was my Critic who helped me connect with my clients by spotting the boxes operating in their lives and teaching me to describe those boxes as strategies without shame. It was my Critic who taught me so much about inner critics that I can hear other people's critics, too, and help them transform those critics into gifts like mine.

My Critic has been instrumental in the writing of this book. It helped me figure out where my Shaming-Fleeing box came from, how and why I built it, what it was made of, how it operated inside me, how it affected my life, and why it was so hard to change. My Critic has held me to my highest standards, insisting that I work through the personal issues that arose during the writing and commit myself to finishing the book. My Critic has, in fact, been quite vocal in its opposition whenever I thought about giving up. I would not have written this book without the unceasing help of my Critic, and I'm enormously grateful for this richly rewarding experience.

Chapter 17

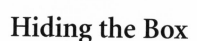

Hiding the Box

From the moment I decided to leave my Shaming-Fleeing box for good, my Risk Manager tried to stop me. At first, I didn't know that it was my Risk Manager causing the trouble. I didn't know that I *had* a Risk Manager.

The first time it tried to stop me, I only knew that I wanted my voice back, and I suddenly found myself trying to reason with a bully and getting nowhere. The facilitators asked me what was at risk for me to get my voice back, and the risk became clear: I was afraid I would get killed. It turned out that I had been afraid of that since I was a child. They acknowledged what a big risk that was and honored my reasons for stifling myself. They helped me see that I was already getting killed inside my head so I might as well take the risk and get my voice back.

The next time my Risk Manager tried to stop me, I knew only that I wanted to receive a blessing, and my mind unexpectedly wandered off. The risk in letting the blessing in was that it might go away again and I would lose hope. The facilitators acknowledged what a big risk that was and honored my reasons for not letting in support. They helped me see that I was already giving up hope so I might as well take the risk and let the blessing in.

Not until the third time my Risk Manager tried to stop me did I become aware that it existed. I wanted my power back to fuel a creative life. I was all ready to go for it when suddenly my mouth went dry and I couldn't speak. Since I couldn't tell them what the risk was, the facilitators had no alternative but to talk to my Risk Manager directly. The risk was that I might believe I had evil inside and feel I couldn't trust anything about myself. The facilitators acknowledged what a huge risk that was. They honored my Risk Manager for protecting me from that risk and suggested that it might even have saved my life. They called my Risk Manager a wise voice and solicited its perspective and advice. They asked my Risk Manager to remain a part of the process and stay nearby in case they needed to talk to it again.

Although I had not known my Risk Manager was there looking out for me, it had been playing a central role all along. When I was hurt by Dad's ridicule, my Risk Manager advised me to choose the Never Again strategy so I would stay connected to Dad. As life went on, my Risk Manager was vigilant in scanning the horizon for threats. A threat consisted of any situation that even faintly resembled the incident with Dad. Feeling I belonged in a group of girlfriends looked like a threat, and so did creative writing. My Risk Manager did everything in its power to keep me out of groups and silence my creative voice. But it was in constant conflict with the nine-year-old inside the box who never stopped wanting to belong. It repeatedly ignored my Risk Manager's warnings and kept propelling me into groups. Each time I joined a group, my Risk Manager bided its time. When I inevitably blurted out something critical, my Editor shamed me for being critical, and my Risk Manager drilled the point home: that I had made a terrible mistake in thinking this could work, that I wasn't good at groups, that I should leave now and never come back. Shamed by the Editor and chastened by my Risk Manager, I always fled.

When I felt lonely at night in bed, it was my Risk Manager who handed me the pain to hug to my chest. The pain was my love for Dad, though I didn't know it. My Risk Manager had long since helped me forget the incident with Dad. From a Risk Manager's point of view, remembering would only bring up the painful feelings of grief, anger, fear and resignation from that event. Those feelings would likely cause conflict between Dad and me and further threaten my bond with him. My Risk Manager helped me forget that I had ever loved to draw colorful pictures. It kept me from seeing that my box had four walls because they would look familiar and remind me of Dad. It allowed me to see the Editor wall because the Editor had the power to shame me out of a group and demolish my creative writing, which made it my Risk Manager's ally. It was in my Risk Manager's best interests to believe that the box was *about me* so I would not even be tempted to think outside it.

But of course I tried to think outside the box anyway, when the feelings from bouncing off the walls became too painful, or when I saw someone in the world who could write creatively or socialize easily with a group of close friends. To think outside the box, I had only to flip into the In-Your-Face strategy and bound into another group. ("Maybe I've been thinking about this all wrong! Maybe it's not really hard at all!") It seemed so easy to just be different! What I couldn't see, of course, was that it was my nine-year-old self in charge and acting in exactly the way you would expect a nine-year-old to act who had been closed up in a box for years: clueless, immature, saying anything that came into her head. I couldn't connect any more successfully than I had before. Eventually, the box settled back into its original shape, my Editor reemerged, and I felt shamed all over again. I flipped back to my original strategy with my Risk Manager screaming at me, "What were you *thinking?*" It showed me vivid, full color videos of my foolishness until I agreed never, *ever* to try that again. Once I had agreed, my Risk Manager gradually let me forget the incident, and life went on.

From my Risk Manager's point of view, the box was a magnificent success. I didn't belong in any groups, and I did no creative writing!

From the point of view of my nine-year-old self inside the box, and everyone else in my life, the box was a problem. The Risk Manager was resistance they needed to overcome.

"Why are you afraid of groups?" someone would ask me. "If you want to write poetry, why don't you do it? Why are you so afraid? *What are you so worried about?*"

My Risk Manager took questions like these as a personal affront. The more it felt affronted, the more resistant it became to letting me change, and the more it hid from view.

RISK MANAGERS IN HIDING

I've talked to a lot of Risk Managers since becoming fully trained as a facilitator. Most Risk Managers have taken a lot of criticism and become very resistant to change. Many of them, in fact, have become resistant to being seen at all, since they know they're likely to be criticized for resisting change. It's not surprising, then, that some people believe they don't have a Risk Manager at all.

"If I have a Risk Manager," a man named Stewart once asked me, "how is it that bad things still happened to me?"

We were getting coffee during a break in a weekend workshop I was leading. After four years of training, I had become certified as a group facilitator and for private sessions.

I had talked with Stewart at some length before the workshop and knew that he had been beaten by his alcoholic mother as a shall child. In the workshop I had described the Risk Manager as a protector, and he naturally wanted to know why his Risk Manager had not protected him from his mother's beatings.

"I'll bet there was a good reason," I replied. I was sending a message to his Risk Manager that I would honor its reasons, hoping that it would share those reasons with Stewart. "What might have happened to you," I continued, "if you had stood up to your mother and tried to stop her from beating you?"

Stewart thought about it for a minute.

"She was a single mother and an alcoholic," he answered. "I think she was right on the edge of losing it a lot of the time. If I had stood up to her, I think she would have seen me as too much trouble and left me somewhere. She would have abandoned me."

"Were there family members nearby who would have taken you in?" I asked.

Stewart shook his head. "Nobody."

"How old were you when the beatings started?" I asked.

"I was three when my father left," he answered. "I think that's when it started."

"At three years old, do you think you could have made it on your own?"

"No."

"It sounds to me," I said, "as if your survival might have been at risk if she had abandoned you. Is that right?"

"Yes, I guess so."

"Your Risk Manager may have done the only thing it could do for

151

you at that young age," I said. "You had no money, no resources, no family nearby. It couldn't find you another place to live. The one thing it could do was keep you from standing up to her and getting abandoned."

Stewart nodded thoughtfully.

"I invite you to consider," I said, "that your Risk Manager may very well have saved your life."

Stewart looked at me, and I saw sadness well up in his eyes. I was willing to bet that he had been feeling shame all these years about not standing up to his mother. He had probably been thinking of himself as weak and powerless, as I had when I stifled my voice in order to keep from getting killed.

Stewart's Risk Manager had made a very tough choice and decided to allow something bad to happen in order to avoid something even worse. It did what every Risk Manager does: it made the best decision possible based on the available options, and for the best motives imaginable—to help Stewart go on living.

RETURN OF THE RISK MANAGER

Later that afternoon, Stewart stepped into the center of the group to do a process. His childhood strategy of submitting to abuse from his mother was repeating in his romantic relationships with women. He was tired of it and wanted to learn to stand up for himself. He wanted his self-respect back.

A tall woman named Francine played his girlfriend. She pounded one fist into the other and yelled, "I'm the one in charge here! What you want doesn't matter!"

Opposite her stood a thin man named Noah, who was playing Stewart when he submitted instead of standing up for himself. Noah stood meekly with his arms at his sides, asking plaintively, "Why is this happening to me?"

Noah happened to be wearing a black T-shirt. When I asked Stewart if this part had a color, he draped dark blue around Noah's neck so that the black T-shirt still showed beneath it. As Stewart stood back to view the effect, I saw that Noah was black and blue.

Standing next to Stewart at the end of the room, I asked him if the scene looked familiar. He readily recognized Francine as his mother and Noah as himself as a young boy. When I asked him what he wanted to have happen in the scene to help him get his self-respect back, his face looked a bit blank.

"I'm not sure," he said.

"Is there a part of you," I asked, "that finds it hard to trust that this process can work well for you?"

"Yes," he said, turning towards me with a look of longing. I believed it to be his Risk Manager's longing for acknowledgment for all that it had done to help him survive.

"Would you be willing to look around the room," I asked, "and choose someone to play that part of you so I can talk to it directly?"

He asked a man named Rick, who stood up and came forward. I asked Stewart and Rick to switch places and then moved to Stewart's side as he took on the role of his Risk Manager.

"Hi!" I said. "So you're the part of Stewart that finds it hard to trust that this process can work well for him, is that right?"

"Yes," Stewart answered. His whole demeanor had changed. He stood with his arms crossed in front of his chest, his face skeptical. He reminded me of a bouncer at a night club.

"I want to welcome you here," I said. "I'm really glad to have a chance to speak with you directly, and I appreciate your willingness to speak with me." Stewart nodded slightly to let me know he'd heard me.

"I think you're a part of Stewart that's been watching out for him, probably for a long time, is that right?"

"Yes," Stewart said.

"Do you have a sense of how long you've been doing that?" I asked.

"Since his dad left."

"Since his dad left," I repeated. I figured that Stewart's Risk Manager wasn't accustomed to being heard or acknowledged, since Stewart had wondered if it even existed. I was repeating its exact words as a way of signaling that I would listen to every word it said.

"I think Stewart said he was three when his dad left, is that right?" I asked.

"Yes."

"In the years since he was three, I'll bet you've saved him from some pretty risky situations," I said.

"Yes," he replied.

I was very struck with this Risk Manager's toughness. It wasn't going to give me one iota of information more than it wanted to.

"With a mother like this," I said, gesturing at Francine, "I'll bet there were lots of risky situations. Am I right?"

"Yes."

"And maybe not just with his mother but with other people, too. Is that right?"

"Yes," Stewart answered.

"How would you describe your role in Stewart's life?" I asked.

"I help him hang in there and keep taking it," Stewart answered. "I help him stay strong."

"Stewart mentioned his girlfriends," I said. "Is that one place you've helped him hang in there and keep taking it?"

"Yes," he answered. "He's had a couple girlfriends who went ballistic on him. One of them threw things." He looked at me as if wondering what I thought of girlfriends who threw things.

"Wow," I said, raising my eyebrows. "I want to honor you for being willing to talk to me, since I'm a girl, and in the past Stewart has known girls who threw things."

"You're okay," he said.

I wondered if I dared use a little humor. I paused a moment for effect.

"I hardly ever throw things," I said with a sweet smile.

"I'll bet," Stewart answered. "But just in case, I'm keeping my eye on you."

"I'm so glad Stewart's got you looking out for him," I laughed. My job was to win over this very resistant Risk Manager so it would help Stewart get what he wanted.

"Thank you," Stewart said. His shoulders had relaxed somewhat. My evil plan was working.

"Did you help him at other times, too, besides with the girlfriends who threw things?" I asked.

"Yes, I've helped him at work. He's had jobs working for people who have anger issues, who want somebody to yell at because it makes them feel better about themselves."

"So your job is to help him hang in there and keep taking it, from the women he's in relationship with, and from people at work."

"From nut cases out in the world, too," Stewart said. "Last year he was in a fender bender in a parking lot with a guy who got out of his car and started screaming. He looked like the kind of person who would have a gun in his glove compartment, so I told Stewart to keep his mouth shut."

"So you protect him in situations where there's a threat to his physical safety, maybe even to his life."

"Yes."

"And at work, what's the risk there?"

"He might get fired."

"So there you're protecting him from a threat to his financial well-being. Is that right?"

"Yes."

"So it sounds to me like you protect Stewart whenever standing up for himself would not work well. Is that right?"

"That's right," Stewart said.

"And I imagine that started with his mother. Is that right?"

"Yes. It was only going to make matters worse."

"So it sounds to me as if you knew that standing up for himself was only going to make matters worse, and you helped him hang in there and take it and stay strong."

"Yes."

"I want to honor the role you've been playing in Stewart's life," I said. "I'm so glad he's had a part like you looking out for him all this time."

"Thank you," Stewart said. He was very matter-of-fact, as if what he had done was no big deal. This Risk Manager had exactly what Stewart was looking for in his life: the toughness it would take to stand up for himself.

"What might have happened to him if you had not been there?" I asked.

"She would have left him somewhere," Stewart answered. "She did leave him once."

"She left him somewhere?"

"Yes. Left him in a store. Drove away and didn't come back for two hours."

"Wow," I said. "What was that like for him?"

"Scary," he said. "Some nice people in the store stayed with him, but he was scared."

"How old was he when that happened?" I asked.

"Five."

"So this wasn't just some theoretical risk," I said. "You knew she might abandon him because she had done it once before."

"Yes."

"I'll bet you saw how scared he was, and you didn't want that to *ever* happen again."

"Yes."

"It's my belief that a part like you doesn't get acknowledged very often," I went on. "In fact, a part like you often gets criticized, even when it's just doing its job. I wonder if you've ever been criticized for doing your job and keeping Stewart from standing up to his mother."

"Some of his school friends gave him a hard time about it," Stewart said. "One of his girlfriends in high school told him he was weak."

"Weak," I repeated. "I'll tell you how I see this. I think you helped him hang in there and take it and stay strong. Because I think you're a part who would rather *walk through fire* than ever let that little boy get that scared again." I was letting compassion rise in my voice.

For the first time, I saw emotion on Stewart's face.

"That's not what I would call weak," I went on. "In my judgment, Stewart has become a very strong man thanks to your help. Strong enough to take it from his girlfriends, and from people he's worked for who have anger issues, and from the guy in the parking lot last year who might have had a gun. I think it takes a strong person to take that kind of punishment. And Stewart's been taking it ever since he was three years old. That's what I call strength."

Stewart took a big breath. He had unfolded his arms and pulled back his shoulders, so that he appeared taller.

"He could still be stronger," Stewart said, somewhat tentatively, I thought. I heard the faintest hint of weariness in his voice. It was just what I had been waiting for.

"And what's this been like for *you*?" I went on. "What's it been like to keep him from standing up for himself all these years, with his mother and girlfriends and bosses and guys in parking lots?"

"It's been tiring," Stewart said. "I would like to take a break now and again, but I don't know if Stewart is up to the task yet. That's why I brought him here."

"So you brought him here," I said, "so you could be sure he was up to the task before you took a break, so he would never be left unprotected."

"Yes."

"You know," I said, "it's really striking me that you've been like a father to him. Like the father he hasn't had since he was three years old." Stewart looked a bit surprised, but he nodded as if he liked the idea.

"I think that's what a father does," I said. "He finds out what his boy needs and then supports him as he goes for it. And I'll bet you'll be with him every step of the way, because I have seldom seen a more loving Risk Manager than you, keeping him strong all these years, and keeping him from getting abandoned."

"Thank you," he said. His body was looking more relaxed by the minute.

"I would like your help," I said. "I want to make sure that this process works really well for Stewart, so he can learn to stand up for himself, and also so you can take a break now and again. I think you know Stewart really well, much better than I ever could. Would you be willing to continue to stand guard while we do this, and let us know about any risks that come up as he does this? Because I don't want him to do anything that's even a *little* too risky. Would you be willing to do that?"

"Yes." Stewart looked pleased.

"Thanks," I said. "If you see a risk, please let me know, and I'll switch Stewart into you so I can find out from you directly what the risk is and what we need to do to make it safe for Stewart to proceed. I'll keep an eye out for risks, too. When we're done, I would like to check in with you one last time, to make sure everything went okay and nothing else needs to happen. Would that be okay?"

"Yes," Stewart answered. He had stuck his thumbs in his belt. He reminded me of a cowboy waiting to climb onto his horse.

We had permission for Stewart to proceed.

Chapter 18

What Honoring Does

Stewart's Risk Manager had been resisting change for a long time. But it had not always been so resistant. At first, it had acted like a wise friend, counseling him and watching out for him, making sure he never got as scared again as he was when his mother drove off and left him.

As Stewart grew, he began to hear from people around him that he should change. His school friends thought he should stand up to his mother, and his high school girlfriend called him weak. The little boy in Stewart who was in touch with his inborn self-respect was trapped inside a box. As the little boy and the Risk Manager came increasingly into conflict, Stewart's Risk Manager gradually changed in character.

STEWART: I don't like it when Mom hits me. I want my self-respect. But it's scary when she leaves me somewhere.	HIS RISK MANAGER: I know how scared you were when you were alone. I don't ever want you to feel that scared and alone again. I'll help you hang in there and take it, and then you won't be left alone.	
STEWART: My school friends say I should stand up to my mom. I want them to respect me, and I want to respect myself.	HIS RISK MANAGER: If you stand up to her, she might leave you somewhere, and then you'd be alone and scared, remember?	
STEWART: My girlfriend says I'm weak. I want her to respect me. I want my self-respect.	HIS RISK MANAGER: Yeah, I know, but you seem to be forgetting something . . .	
STEWART: My boss has anger issues. I want my self-respect back. But I seem to be stuck in this box . . .	HIS RISK MANAGER: You don't seem to respect what I'm doing here. I'm protecting you!	
STEWART: I don't like it when my girlfriend throws things. I want my self-respect back. I would like to get out of this box now, please.	HIS RISK MANAGER: You really don't get it, do you? If you get out of the box, your girlfriend will leave you, and you'll be alone and scared! What then?!	

STEWART: But it's my self-respect I'm talking about here! I need it, it's an important part of me! Aren't you listening to me?	HIS RISK MANAGER: I'm listening to you, but you're not listening to *me*!	
STEWART: I've just got to get my self-respect back! LET ME OUT!	HIS RISK MANAGER: Over my dead body! You don't remember how scared and alone you felt, but I sure do! I said I would protect you, and that's what I'm going to do whether you like it or not!	

The attitude of Stewart's Risk Manager went through a progression looking something like this:

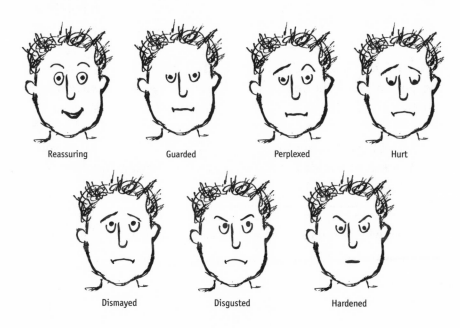

Reassuring   Guarded   Perplexed   Hurt

Dismayed   Disgusted   Hardened

Just as the Risk Manager hardened in response to its conflict with Stewart, so it began to soften when I honored its reasons for resisting change.

First, when I talked to Stewart during the break, he wanted to know why his Risk Manager had not protected him from his mother's beatings. It had not occurred to him before that something worse might have happened if he had stood up to her. Stewart's Risk Manager had supplied this new information.

WHAT I SAID TO STEWART: I'll bet there was a good reason.	THE MESSAGE TO HIS RISK MANAGER: I believe you've had good reasons for the ways you've helped Stewart.
I SAID: What might have happened to Stewart if he had stood up to his mother?	THE MESSAGE TO HIS RISK MANAGER: I believe something terrible might have happened to Stewart if he had not followed your advice.
I SAID: Your Risk Manager might have done the only thing it could do.	THE MESSAGE: I believe you did the best you could with very limited options.
I SAID: I invite you to consider that your Risk Manager may have saved your life.	THE MESSAGE: I believe you are a life-saving protector.

Later, when I honored Stewart's Risk Manager directly, it supplied new information. His mother had left Stewart alone in a store when he was five.

I SAID: I want to welcome you here.	THE MESSAGE: I consider you a valued part of this process.
I SAID: I appreciate your willingness to speak with me.	THE MESSAGE: You have rights, including the right to refuse to speak to me.
I SAID: I'll bet you've saved Stewart from some pretty risky situations.	THE MESSAGE: I think you you are a good guy, not a bad guy.
I SAID: With a mother like his, I'll bet there were lots of risky situations.	THE MESSAGE: Watching out for Stewart must have been a lot of work for you.
I SAID: I think you would rather suffer yourself than ever let Stewart suffer like that again.	THE MESSAGE: I believe you are noble, strong compassionate and devoted.
I SAID: I think you know Stewart really well, much better than I ever could.	THE MESSAGE: You're an expert, and I value your expertise.
I SAID: I don't want him to do anything that's even a little too risky.	THE MESSAGE: I really care about Stewart's safety, and I don't want him to ignore your warnings.
I SAID: I'll keep an eye out for risks, too.	THE MESSAGE: I'll work with you on this. You don't have to do it all by yourself.

For the Risk Manager, the reaction to being honored goes something like this:

Skeptical	Waiting	Surprised	Touched
You're okay with my not trusting?	I'm waiting to see what you're going to do.	You mean you *want* me here?	It feels so good to be acknowledged!

Relieved	Eager	Ally
You mean I can still help?	Sure, I would love to help!	Listen, here's what happened a long time ago . . .

THE RISK MANAGER AS ALLY

Stewart's Risk Manager didn't want to be constantly resisting his desire for self-respect any more than Stewart wanted to stay in the box. His Risk Manager wanted to play its original role of compassionate advisor.

When Stewart let me talk to his Risk Manager directly, he made the choice to believe that there could have been good reasons why he didn't stand up to his mother. In effect, he was saying to his Risk Manager, "I know now that it wasn't your fault that Mom beat me. You're not bad, you're good. You were just doing your job and protecting me. Thank you for all your help. I'm grown up now, and I can take it from here."

When Stewart was no longer in conflict with his Risk Manager, the energy he was expending on that conflict was available for other things in his life, such as his relationship with his girlfriend. When Stewart started working with his Risk Manager instead of against it, their combined efforts were formidable. His greatest reward, though, in my opinion, was not the things he accomplished but the person he *became*. His new self-respect was evident to the people around him, and they responded to him differently. His relationship with his girlfriend deepened, and they are now married. He changed jobs and is now working for a boss who respects him. Best of all, Stewart now respects himself. The little boy inside the box grew up as life intended. Of course, there were trials and errors along the way, as there are for every boy as he grows into a man.

At the end of his process, I invited Stewart to go inside himself and feel his experience of the Risk Manager in his body. He felt it as a steely blue shield inside his chest. A few weeks after the workshop, I got an email from Stewart saying he had fashioned a shield out of some old sheet metal and painted it a steely blue. The shield now held an honored place in his home alongside other sacred objects. Whenever he contemplated making a change in his life, he placed the shield on a chair opposite his own and spoke to it as if he were speaking to his Risk Manager. Then he switched places and sat in the Risk Manager's chair, holding the shield to his chest, and giving his Risk Manager's perspective on the proposed change.

Stewart found a way to assess upcoming risks so that he could make more conscious decisions as he went forward. His Risk Manager became his wisest ally, his strongest protector, his most compassionate source of support, and his most trusted companion. And it will never die or leave him because it's a part of him.

Chapter 19

Honoring Your Risk Manager

Whenen I honored Stewart's Risk Manager, I conveyed the message that, in my opinion, there were good reasons for Stewart's box and for his resistance to changing it.

Now, I'm going to give you the same opportunity.

MEDICAL DISCLAIMER

In this exercise, I will give you an opportunity to have your Risk Manager honored the way I did with Stewart. This exercise may be challenging for you emotionally. This exercise is not a substitute for therapy or medical treatment. If you are under the care of a therapist or physician, please discuss this exercise with them before proceeding. If you find yourself feeling uncomfortable or resistant at any time, feel free to stop the exercise.

PREPARING THE SPACE

For best results, please take the following steps to prepare the space before starting this exercise. By "space," I mean both your physical location and your emotional space, or frame of mind.

1) This exercise is optional. Do it only if you want to. Forcing yourself will only result in more resistance from your Risk Manager and, consequently, will tend to do more harm than good. If you find yourself feeling uncomfortable or resistant during the exercise, please stop and skip ahead to Chapter 20 instead.

2) *Do not* do this exercise while driving a car or operating machinery, or while doing anything involving physical or emotional risk.

3) Set aside enough time to complete the exercise before returning to your regular life. You may want to set aside an hour or more.

4) Do this exercise in a safe, private place where you won't be interrupted. Unplug the phone and draw the shades if that feels right to you. If there's an unavoidable risk of interruption, decide before you begin what you will do if an interruption occurs.

5) You may find that tears come up during this exercise, so have some tissues handy. Crying may mean that your Risk Manager is feeling a wave of relief. If you can allow that relief to flow through you in the form of tears, it will aid the process of transforming your Risk Manager into an ally.

6) You can invite someone to be with you as a support, or you might prefer to be alone.

7) This exercise invites you to move physically, because movement can add powerful learning to your experience. If movement isn't possible for you, please do what's right for you.

8) Have a pen or pencil ready to write about your experience in the spaces provided. You may want to have a journal or writing pad available as well.

9) During the last part of the exercise, you might enjoy having some tender, compassionate music playing. If so, set that up before you begin.

EXERCISE

The purpose of this exercise is to give you a taste of what it's like to step into your Risk Manager and have your Risk Manager honored.

This is what will happen. First, I'll ask you to think about what becoming practically shameless might mean for you. Next, I'll describe the Risk Manager part of you so you'll know what I'm talking about. I'll ask if you're willing to step into your Risk Manager. If you say yes, I'll ask you to step into it. I'll talk to your Risk Manager directly. I'll ask if it has a message of support for you. Then I'll switch you back into your regular self and give you an opportunity to hear that message of support from the other side, if there was one. If you choose, I'll help you anchor your experience in your body so you can access it more easily again later. I'll explain what we just did. The whole thing might take about fifteen minutes.

When I talk to your Risk Manager about you, I'll refer to you with a short dotted line like this: .... Some people find it easiest to write their name on the short dotted line wherever it appears before they start the exercise.

Becoming Practically Shameless

Picture yourself becoming practically shameless. What might becoming practically shameless mean for you? You can jot down some ideas here:

_____

_____

_____

Locating Your Risk Manager

The part I'm calling your Risk Manager is the part of you that *finds it hard to trust that you could become practically shameless.* If you're not sure what I mean, here are some other ways to describe your Risk Manager:

- The part of you that stays on the lookout, like a radar operator.
- The part of you that stands guard, like a guardian angel, to make sure nothing hurts you.
- The part of you that's walking one step ahead of you, like a scout.

If you think you have a Risk Manager, I want you to imagine that your Risk Manager is nearby, perhaps sitting right next to you.

Stepping In

Now I would like you to "step into" your Risk Manager so I can talk to that part of you directly.

By stepping into it, I mean shifting an inch on your chair, or sitting in a slightly different position, so that you're "in" the role of your Risk Manager instead of in your regular self. If you imagined your Risk Manager in another place in the room, stepping into it might mean moving to that place in the room and taking this book with you.

Would you be willing to "step into" your Risk Manager?

If the answer is yes, please do that. Shift an inch, or sit in a different position, or move to another place in the room where your Risk Manager is right now.

When you're there, please continue reading.

Hi!

So you are ....'s Risk Manager, is that right?

Welcome! I appreciate your willingness to speak with me.

I think you are the part of .... that stays on the lookout for things that might be risky. I think you are a wise voice that tries to keep .... safe.

I'll bet you have been on the lookout for a long time. And I'll bet that you have saved .... from some risky situations.

What are some risky situations you have saved .... from?

And what might have happened to .... if you had not been there?

_____

_____

I wonder if you might even have saved ....'s life. Am I right? Want to say how?

_____

_____

I want to honor you for the role you've been playing in ....'s life.

In this book, I have described some ways people can become practically shameless by healing their shame and transforming the boxes that have trapped them. And I asked .... to jot down a few ideas about what it might mean to become practically shameless.

What might be at risk for .... to become practically shameless?

_____

_____

I'm glad that .... has a part like you, watching out to make sure nothing happens that's too risky. Because I would not want .... to do anything that's just too risky. I think of you as my ally here, someone who knows .... far better than I ever could, who can help me make sure that doesn't happen.

It's been my experience that a part like you usually isn't acknowledged for the valuable role you play. On the contrary, I think a part like you sometimes gets criticized for doing its job. People might have called you "a skeptic" or "too cautious" or even "a chicken." They might have asked you, "What are you so worried about?"

And I think you knew EXACTLY what there was to worry about, and you stayed on the job.

I want to honor you for that. I'm really glad you have been there for ...., standing guard.

And I want to ask you something. Would you be willing to stay on the lookout while .... thinks about becoming practically shameless in the days and weeks to come?

Thank you for letting me speak to you. In a moment, I'm going to invite you to step back into ....

Before I do that, however, I want to offer you an opportunity you may not have had before: to send .... a message of support. Because .... may not have known that you were there, on the lookout, standing guard. Do you think it would make a difference to ...., the next time life gets hard, to feel your presence and hear a message of support from you?

If so, would you like to send .... a message of support?

If yes, you can do it in whatever way feels right to you. You might have words, or you might have a message to send straight from your heart. You might want to put on some nice music as you do this.

Write your message of support here.

If you would rather not send a message of support, that's fine, too.

And now, I want you to step back into .... so you can hear this from the other side.

Back in Yourself

Shift back to your original position, or move back to your original place in the room, so that you're back in your regular self.

Take a minute to come back into your regular self.

I've been talking with a part of you I'll refer to as your Risk Manager. You might have a different name for this part of you. Whatever name you've got for it is the right one for you.

I've asked your Risk Manager if it would be willing to stay on the lookout as you think about healing shame in the hours and days to come.

I also asked your Risk Manager if it would like to send you a message of support. If it sent you a message, I would like you to hear the message from the other side.

When you're ready, I invite you to read aloud the message of support written on the previous page.

And see if you can let it in.

Take a moment to notice how this feels.

How does this feel, to hear this message of support? How does it feel to know that you have a part like this that's looking out for you?

It feels:

_____

_____

Is this a feeling you would like to remember? If yes, I'll help you anchor it. Anchoring will make it more accessible to you later.

Anchoring

Close your eyes, and go inside yourself for a moment.

Is there a certain place in your body where this feeling lives, this feeling of support from your Risk Manager, and from knowing that you have a part like this that's looking out for you?

*The place in my body:*_____

And when this feeling is in that place in your body, what is it like? Does it have a color, or a shape, or a size?

Its color: _____

Its shape: _____

Its size: _____

Now look at what you just described. Does this description, with its color or shape or size, remind you of something? For example, if you described it as big and gold, could it be big and gold like the sun? If you described it as broad and silver, is it broad and silver like a shield?

It reminds me of: _____

_____

Finally, go inside to that place in your body one more time. Focus on this feeling, in that place in your body, this feeling with this color or shape or size you described, this feeling that reminded you of something. And ask yourself, "What wonderful thing does this feeling have to say to me, *about* me, something that might start with 'I' or 'I am'?" For example, it might say something like, "I take care of myself" or "I am strong."

It says: _____

_____

Your Risk Manager as Advisor

Would you like to keep in touch with your Risk Manager?

If yes, picture for a moment the description you gave of the feeling inside you, and what it reminded you of.

Is there an object you own that could represent your Risk Manager?

An object: _____

_____

If you don't currently have an object you could use, is there one you could easily get?

I could get: _____

_____

There is one more thing I want to say.

I believe your Risk Manager is a valuable advisor. And I believe it's up to *you* to decide what happens. You're the one in charge, not your Risk Manager, and not me.

I encourage you to consider staying in touch with your Risk Manager and getting its advice on changes you want to make in your life. When you think of a change you want to make, step into your Risk Manager just as you did during this exercise. Then ask, "What might be at risk for me to make this change?" Listen to the risks. Listen for the good reasons that those risks exist, reasons from your past experiences. And remember, it's your job to make the final decisions.

Is there anything else about this exercise that you would like to remember? If so, you can write it here.

_____

_____

_____

_____

_____

_____

_____

_____

_____

_____

_____

_____

Chapter 20

Practically Shameless

My life today is much happier than it was back in 1995 when I first encountered Shadow Work. I know myself really well and like myself as a person, most of the time. I treat myself well and believe I am worthy of love, most of the time. I think of my feelings as rivers that want simply to run through me and reach the ocean and I let them do that, most of the time. I feel connected to a circle of close friends and family members, both women and men. I feel connected to the Divine, most of the time.

I keep in touch with my Risk Manager. When I first became aware of having a Risk Manager, I thought of it as a male figure because I couldn't imagine a female figure protecting me effectively—another legacy, I believe, of my mother's inability to stand up to angry men. Today my Risk Manager is decidedly female, and I listen to her warnings, most of the time.

I make my living helping people and get a deep satisfaction from it. In a group, I'm sometimes able to see what others cannot, and I get a lot of satisfaction from that, too. At its farthest reaches, Shadow Work becomes shamanism, where I begin to see life in images and symbols, and the spiritual plane becomes more real than the physical.

I still eat too much, and I'm working on that.

My second marriage ended when it appeared that our ideas of marriage were too different to reconcile. I resolved to go through the divorce process without putting anything in a box and it went quite well. I like my ex-husband very much as a person and we're quite comfortable with each other.

My daughter and I still watch the occasional movie together, but we spend most our time together talking and sharing, often at a deep level. We know each other well. As she takes on life as an adult, I have no doubt she will become as important a part of my support system as I have been of hers.

ABOUT SHAME

Shame still comes up for me sometimes. That's both the good news and the bad news. Let me explain.

Occasionally, shame from my Shaming-Fleeing box comes up again. It means to me that my Risk Manager has sensed a new risk that she is not ready to take and she wants to keep me safe in a box. Once again, I'm bouncing off the walls: I'm bad, I'm not okay the way I am, I'm not a loving person, I'm powerless to change.

But I have transformed the box and now I know the way out. I know it not just with my mind but through my experience, so the knowing is in my cells. As I bounce against the Editor wall, I know from experience that I'm not bad at all. If even a predator like the Editor isn't bad, then there are no bad people, only wounded ones. There's something important for me to learn from the new risk I've encountered, about some part of me that believes it's bad but isn't. When I free that part of me from prison, what felt momentarily like a wall again becomes a portal.

The same happens with the other walls. I ask for support from the Divine and feel its unconditional love and compassion for me. I know from experience that I'm inherently lovable and can feel it in my chest, gold like the sun. I call on my Warrior to set a boundary to protect myself as I face the new risk and feel new strength for meeting the unknown. I am powerful once again. When I see that I'm in a box, I know from experience that I built it as a way of loving Dad. I have felt in my body how much love it takes to live with a painful box like this. Each time I feel the river of love in my chest, the river dredges a deeper channel so I feel more deeply.

Being practically shameless means reducing the cycle time, from feeling shame to knowing you're not bad, to feeling compassion for yourself, to feeling what a loving person you are for having carried that shame, to feeling good about yourself again. I lived in my Shaming-Fleeing box for nearly forty years. When I feel the shame of that box today, I can get back to feeling good about myself within days, within hours, within minutes, sometimes within seconds.

The good news is that I'll never be entirely free of shame. Each time I feel shame, I undergo a growth process, learn something new to like about myself, feel more compassion for myself for having been hurt, see myself as more loving for having carried the hurt for so long, and feel my strength and power for healing it.

Shame is what we feel when one of the portals hardens into a wall. That hardening process gives us the impression that we're separate from the Divine, but that's not actually the case. The Divine is always with us and in us. One of the greatest gifts we get from the Divine is the feeling that we're separate, which allows us to become real beings who can return the Divine's love. In hardening, we become real and unique, like a molten planet whose crust is cooling. The crust will come to support plant life, and each plant that grows will absorb the sun's light, make food from it, and grow. When it grows, it will absorb more of the sun's light, make more food from it, and grow some more. It will develop a relationship with the sunlight. When the crust supports animal life, each animal will respond to the Divine flowing through it in the form of instincts and feelings. When the crust supports human life, each human will have the choice to be in conscious relationship with the Divine. That's why we were created: the Divine is love, and love seeks to love and be loved in return. The Divine created us so that it could have someone to love and be loved by in return.

The box is the reason we're here. It's the farthest thing possible from a mistake.

Imagine transforming a solid, windowless wall into a doorway through which you can see life as you'd like it to be. Imagine that you can walk through that doorway and become the person you've always known you could be.

You can do more than imagine it. You can do it. I know you can because I did it.

THE HERO'S JOURNEY

Becoming practically shameless is to take what Joseph Campbell called the hero's journey. A hero sets out on a quest, finds something new that no one ever found before and then brings it back to share it with the world. When you play the role of hero, there's no way of knowing exactly where the quest will take you or what you will bring home.

Each time I begin working on a new issue, I picture myself stepping onto a roller coaster as it is resting at the station. As the machinery drags the car slowly up to the top of the plunge, its crank-crank-crank-crank resonates with the jitters in my stomach.

To begin the journey, all it takes is you, right now, in this moment, saying, "My patterns stop here, with me. I choose not to pass on to my children the ways in which I was hurt. Where I have already done so, I will heal those hurts in myself, and using the insight and compassion I gain, I will share the truth with my children when they are grown enough to hear it. As they grow further, I will help them heal from the ways in which I've hurt them when they hear the call to do so."

If it's your time for a journey, I believe that the Divine will let you know. If something happens to you repeatedly, you may be receiving invitations to a hero's journey. It is your cue to take that first step onto the roller coaster. It's waiting at the station, right now.

When you take the hero's journey, you will learn things no one else has ever learned because no one else has had exactly your experiences. You will break new ground. That learning may well turn out to be the most important reason you were born.

THE RIVER SITTER

When I first became acquainted with the four archetypes in 1995, I was quite captivated with their vivid manifestations in the Arthurian legends: Arthur the Sovereign, Merlin the Magician, Lancelot the Warrior and Guinevere the Lover. I was particularly thrilled to feel my Lancelot holding its own sword and shield, perhaps because of my dream about Dad and his swords. As with my Risk Manager, I thought of my Sovereign, Magician and Warrior as masculine figures because I was so out of touch with my own femininity.

Over time, I've come to see the archetypes in myself somewhat differently. I picture my Sovereign as more like a religious figure than I would have felt comfortable with at that time, after my years of atheism. I most often picture my Sovereign standing tranquilly with arms outstretched in blessing. It is sometimes male, sometimes female, sometimes fatherly, sometimes motherly, sometimes more like a grandparent.

My Warrior is definitely female and of the four, most akin to the wild woman in Dr. Clarissa Pinkola Estes' inspiring book, *Women Who Run with the Wolves*. I picture my Warrior most often in the forest hunting for game, treading silently on dirt paths, protecting my territory from invaders. When aroused, she becomes a mother grizzly bear standing on its hind feet roaring in the face of whoever has disrespected my boundaries.

My Magician is an old wise woman who lives in a simple hut on the outskirts of my realm, at the edge of a dark forest. When I feel afraid, I run to her. I sit in her hut learning how to read the wind and the planets and the behavior of birds and animals.

My Lover is sometimes the seductive dancer bumping and grinding in skin-tight clothes, sometimes a dramatic painter splashing colors wildly on a vast canvas. I notice her sometimes when I'm helping a client anchor an image inside their body; I tend to wave my arms around as if painting the image in the air. My Lover can also be the child in me, the curly-headed girl with skinny legs hiking in the mountains, leaping onto rocks in midstream, following the tiny trails that lead off from the main path, building dams and bridges in a stream out of stones, sticks—and mud.

In fact, mud has become another gift. I love exploring Native American animal medicine and its many messages from animals and birds. My totems include squirrel, bear and frog, and it is frog who enjoys the mud. For frog, mud is a salve and an antidote to fear. Frog sits on a riverbank watching the river flowing by, listening for the dropping of rain and watching for the patterns it makes in the mud.

Appendix

The Shadow Work Model

The Shadow Work Model was created in the early 1990s by Cliff Barry while he was living in Madison, Wisconsin.

Since the mid-1980s, Cliff had been leading seminars for married couples with his first wife, Wendy. Cliff was an ordained minister but no longer had a congregation and felt that his calling was to help couples strengthen and deepen their relationships. He was also leading retreat weekends for men through an organization called the ManKind Project.

As he worked with people, Cliff relied on his experience and intuition to determine the issue a person was facing and how he might help. He found himself wishing for a model that would help guide him and ensure that he was seeing the issue objectively. In his search for a model that would suit the kind of work he wanted to do, he came across a book by Jungian analyst Robert Moore and Douglas Gillette titled *King, Warrior, Magician, Lover: Rediscovering the Archetypes of the Mature Masculine*. Moore's and Gillette's book suggested that the male personality had a four-directional foundation, like a map.

Although Cliff came to see the four archetypes somewhat differently than Moore and Gillette did, he agreed with them that people think in four directions. When we want to get somewhere, we use the four directions on a compass. We use four-sided maps that define the territory across which we travel. With just four directions, it's possible to go anywhere.

When he compared his experiences in working with couples to Moore's and Gillette's four-directional foundation, Cliff found that it could serve as the basis for a new model that could help both men and women. He used the same names for three of the archetypal foundations—Lover, Warrior, and Magician—and renamed the fourth, substituting "Sovereign" for "King."

Starting with Carl G. Jung's notion of the human shadow, and the straightforward imagery of Robert Bly portraying the shadow as a bag hung over one shoulder, Cliff built a working model that mapped out both personal and relationship issues in four directions. It also suggested techniques for addressing them.

With Mary Ellen Whalen (then Blandford), his partner at the time, Cliff came across other systems of four that overlaid on the same four-directional foundation. These other systems helped provide additional clues to the issue a person was facing. One of these systems was the four ancient elements—earth, air, fire and water—which matched up well with Warrior, Magician, Sovereign and Lover, respectively. For example, an issue about territory, which is a partition of earth, is a clue that Warrior energy is in shadow.

Other systems of four include the four human emotions in the work of John Bradshaw (anger, fear, joy and sadness) and the four family roles in alcoholic families (rebel, mascot, hero and lost child) illuminated in the work of Sharon Wegscheider-Cruse on addiction and recovery.

Cliff and Mary Ellen began applying the new model to their work with couples and individuals. It quickly became clear that the new model was deeply transformative and useful in many different areas of life.

Since its development, the Shadow Work Model has emerged as a comprehensive and extremely useful facilitation map for both group and individual work. The Model also builds upon, among other influences: the metaphor work of David Grove; the "guts" work of Ron Hering; the Voice Dialogue system of Hal and Sidra Stone; the theology of Emmanuel Swedenborg; and techniques borrowed from Gestalt psychotherapy, Accelerated Learning, Bio-Energetics, and family systems theory. In recent years, Cliff has explored additional systems that overlay well on the four archetypes, including paradigms in physics and qualities in the nine Enneagram personality types.

As of this writing, retreats and trainings employing the Shadow Work Model have been held in fifteen countries on six continents. The Model's concepts and techniques have been incorporated into the work done by corporations and consulting groups, community and religious organizations, and initiations for both men and women.

THE MODEL IN DETAIL

The Magician

Purpose: . . . . .Guidance through detachment, seeing options

Masculine/feminine: . . . . . . .Cooking by recipe/Cooking by taste

Element: . . . . .Air

Family role: . . . . .Clown, Mascot, Comedian, Trickster

Gateway emotion: . . . . .Fear opens to Magician

Animal instinct: . . . . .Predator

Shadows: . . . . .Dense/rigid (too little Magician energy): "I don't know" or Fragmented (too much Magician energy): "I'm confused"

Deep wound: . . . ."I'm bad"

The tool: . . . . .Look at the scene from a split

The Sovereign

Purpose: . . . . .Motivation through esteem

Masculine/feminine: . . . . . . .Seeing the vision/Blessing and
supporting the follow-through

Element: . . . . .Fire

Family role: . . . . .Hero, Little Parent, Caretaker

Gateway emotion: . . . . .Joy opens to Sovereign

Animal instinct: . . . . .Alpha male or female

Shadows: . . . . .Shy (too little Sovereign energy):
"I can't, it's too hard, I'm tired" or
Shiny (too much Sovereign energy):
"I can ace it"

Deep wound: . . . ."I'm not good enough"

The tool: . . . . .Bring support from an ideal figure

The Lover

Purpose: . . . . .Connection through feeling

Masculine/feminine: . . . . . . .Spirit looking up/Soul looking down

Element: . . . . .Water

Family role: . . . . .Lost child, the quiet but deep one

Gateway emotion: . . . . .Grief opens to Lover

Animal instinct: . . . . .Bonding

Shadows: . . . . .Dry/Stoic (too little Lover energy):
"I can't get at it" or Overflowing
(too much Lover energy): "It's
getting me"

Deep wound: . . . ."I don't love right"

The tool: . . . . .Work in the body, possibly with a
metaphor

The Warrior

Purpose: . . . . .Power and service through boundaries

Masculine/feminine: . . . . . . .Offense/Defense

Element: . . . . .Earth

Family role: . . . . .Rebel, Scapegoat
Gateway emotion: . . . . .Anger opens to Warrior
Animal instinct: . . . . .Territory
Shadows: . . . . .Flaky/Victim (too little Warrior energy):
"Please, no conflict or separation"
or Savage/Defensive (too much Warrior
energy): "You can't get me"
Deep wound: . . . ."I don't exist apart from you"
The tool: . . . . .Set a boundary

THE SIXTEEN BOXES

As I explained in Chapter 14, a box we build is really a strategy, chosen from among the strategies available. Some boxes represent Never Again strategies while others represent In-Your-Face strategies. We experience each pair of strategies as a loop that repeats over and over in our lives. We spend most of our time at one end of that loop, in the strategy that worked best in our early environment. But each end of the loop is an uncomfortable extreme, and we don't stay there forever. Forces inside and outside us build up and propel us to the other end of the loop. It is when we zoom to the loop's other end that we feel a breath of fresh air and believe that we are "thinking outside the box." The box is still there, however, awaiting our inevitable return.

When we're in a box that represents a Never Again strategy, forces inside us—natural urges to express all of who we are, and our feelings about having to hide parts of us from the world—build up until an explosion of sorts propels us to the other end of the loop.

When we're in a box that represents an In-Your-face strategy, forces inside us—depletion, and our feelings about having to "keep it up" all the time—lead to an implosion of sorts that propels us to the other end of the loop.

Whichever box we're in, we unconsciously invite people into our lives to play the opposing role. One of the many reasons we do this is to continue loving the person who originally hurt us.

Viewing the shadow as boxes connected by loops is my own interpretation of the Shadow Work Model. Thinking of the shadow as a box was not my own invention, however; Shadow Work facilitators have long referred to a person's issue as "the box" in another kind of Sovereign blessing process called a God-Split.

Carl Jung himself referred to a box in *Memories, Dreams, Reflections* when he told of coming back to life after nearly dying from a stroke.

> *In reality, a good three weeks were still to pass before I could truly make up my mind to live again. I could not eat because all food repelled me. The view of city and mountains from my sick-bed seemed to me like a painted curtain with black holes in it, or a tattered sheet of newspaper full of photographs that meant nothing. Disappointed, I thought, "Now I must return to the 'box system' again." For it seemed to me as if behind the horizon of the cosmos a three-dimensional world had been artificially built up, in which each person sat by himself in a little box. And now I should have to convince myself all over again that this was important! Life and the whole world struck me as a prison, and it bothered me beyond measure that I should again be finding all that quite in order. I had been so glad to shed it all, and now it had come about that I—along with everyone else—would again be hung up in a box by a thread.*

Neither was it my idea originally to characterize "shadows" as portions of the shadow as a whole. Jung described the shadow as a vast ocean, an image that is somewhat overwhelming and that leaves some people wondering where on earth to start. The traditional answer has been psychoanalysis using dream interpretation and active imagination over a period of years and at huge expense. It was Cliff's brilliant idea to "chunk" the shadow into its various manifestations in specific behaviors and beliefs, categorized by archetype. With this innovation, he quickly learned that his new model could help someone change a specific behavior or belief within a matter of hours.

What my view of shadow as the box shares with the Model itself is the belief that every shadow—every box—was a necessary strategy that helped you survive earlier in your life. It helped you *go on* from a painful experience. There is, therefore, no need to feel shame about anything you have trapped inside a box.

In fact, your shadow says many good things about you: that you loved someone who hurt you, that you trusted someone enough to be hurt, that you were faithful to someone and adopted their beliefs about you, and that you obediently permitted your identity to be shaped by your experience in service to your family system.

Those familiar with Jung's work will recognize in my description of the shadow what Jung termed the personal unconscious. Jung posited three levels of the human unconscious: the personal, the social, and the collective. To distinguish them using Shadow Work terminology, the personal unconscious contains the shadows of an individual person resulting from that individual's own life experiences; the social unconscious contains shadows shared by the members of a society, culture, institution or other group by virtue of their membership in the group; and the collective unconscious contains shadows common to all human beings.

While the Shadow Work Model nominally addresses itself to the personal unconscious by starting with an individual's wants and risks and then tracing those wants and risks back to early personal experiences, it is not unusual for social and collective shadows to appear in an individual's inner play, and in my experience they are interpreted as such by Shadow Work facilitators. For example, as a teenager I perceived certain attitudes toward women in the church in which I was raised, and a social shadow I called "the Church" has appeared as a player at times in my work. Similarly, initiation into adulthood is an archetypal need in every human being, meaning its source lies in the collective unconscious. Since most cultures in the modern world no longer consciously initiate young people, that need is often expressed unconsciously instead in behaviors that initiate adulthood: pregnancy, alcohol abuse, criminal activity, and service in the armed forces.

Magician Boxes

Each of the four archetypes has two sides: one directed outward toward the world, the other directed inward. Picture one of the portals I described in Chapter 8, and you'll notice that you can walk through a portal from the inside or the outside. The Shadow Work Model refers to these two sides as the masculine and feminine aspects of the archetype, respectively.

When we get hurt and realize that part of us is not welcome, an archetypal part of us goes into a box. Since each side of an archetype can result in a loop between two boxes, there are four boxes per archetype.

The Shaming-Fleeing box described throughout this book is an example of the **Predator-Prey** loop, probably the darkest of all the loops and the one most readily recognized as "the shadow" even by people who are not very familiar with the term. When I shamed my friends, I was on the Predator end of the loop, and when I flipped to the Prey end, I fled from groups in fear.

The Predator and Prey boxes are strategies for going on from some form of *predation*. People who have been abused have usually had the Predator-Prey loop operating in many ways in their lives. When the abuse occurred, they had a choice between the Predator strategy, taking control by becoming a perpetrator, and the Prey strategy, taking control by trusting no one.

The **Dogmatic** and **Scattered** boxes are strategies for going on from *attacks on what we know*. By the Dogmatic box I mean a narrow-mindedness that insists on the existence of only one right answer. By the Scattered box I mean its opposite, a surplus of options generally swirling around and creating confusion and fragmentation of thought. Each is a strategy for continuing to learn, the Dogmatic by learning only about the one right option, the Scattered by learning in an unfocused way that leaves no target for attack. The original cast of *Saturday Night Live* often played with this loop, with Gilda Radner and Lorraine Newman playing scattered roles like Roseanne Rosannadanna and Dan Akroyd in a dogmatic role calling fellow commentator Jane Curtin an "ignorant slut."

All Magician boxes tell us what trusting beings we are. We are so trusting that we can be preyed upon by those we love and trust what we're taught even when it disagrees with our own inner knowing. In transforming a Magician box, we learn to trust life and ourselves. With this learning, we become able to create safety for others and follow our own internal guidance.

Sovereign Boxes

The **Grandstanding** and **Shrinking Violet** boxes are strategies for going on from *conditional love*, i.e., from hearing the message that we aren't worthy of love the way we are. By Grandstanding I mean the grandiosity that wants all the attention in the room. By the Shrinking

Violet, I mean its opposite, a shyness that shrinks from the limelight. Each is a strategy for earning love, Grandstanding by demanding attention, the Shrinking Violet by staying small and not asking for much. The *Peanuts* comic strip shows us the loop between these two boxes most strikingly when grandstanding Lucy betrays Charlie Brown, the shrinking violet, when she pulls away the football just as he prepares to kick it.

The **Zealot** and **Apathetic** boxes are strategies for going on from *neglect and lack of nurture*. By the Zealot I mean a super-motivation that demands perfection in service of an idealized goal. By the Apathetic I mean its opposite, a lack of motivation that stops caring. Each is a strategy for finding motivation to care for ourselves, the Zealot by being perfect, the Apathetic by "looking out for number one." Charles Dickens' story *A Christmas Carol* is about the loop between these two boxes. Ebenezer Scrooge zealously acquires wealth, in the process sacrificing his personal life and caring for no one but himself.

All Sovereign boxes tell us how profoundly we believe in and model ourselves on those we admire. In transforming a Sovereign box, we learn to believe in a Divine and in ourselves. With this learning, we become a beacon of belief and acceptance for those around us.

Lover Boxes

The **Wanton** and **Diehard** boxes are strategies for going on from *inappropriate relationship*. By the Wanton I mean the serial lover who carves notches on the bedpost but is incapable of real intimacy. By the Diehard I mean its opposite, the partner who clings to a piece of paper to prove there's a relationship even when it's long since died from lack of feeling. Each is a strategy for feeling like a loving person, the Wanton by compulsively taking lovers, the Diehard by clinging to relationships even when they're empty. The time-honored story of the sailor with a girl in every port and his lonely but devoted wife at home is about this loop.

The **Overwrought** and **Stoic** boxes are strategies for going on from *alienation* or attacks on what we feel. By Overwrought I mean a surplus of emotion bordering on or reaching hysteria. By the Stoic I mean its opposite, emotional shutdown. Each is a strategy for gaining entrance in order to belong, the Overwrought by compulsively expressing feelings, the Stoic by stuffing them. Romantic dramas and comedies enjoy playing with this loop. Romeo is one example of the Overwrought lover whose emotions overflow and lead to murder, and Cyrano de Bergerac is a Stoic who can express his true feelings for Roxanne only in writing. Jane Austen's novel *Sense and Sensibility* contrasts the often-overwrought Marianne with her sensibly stoic sister, Elinor.

All Lover boxes tell us how deeply we love and need to connect with those around us. We learn to love in the way our loved ones did, even if it wasn't what our own feelings and sexuality would dictate. In transforming a Lover box, we learn what it means to be human at the deepest level. With this learning we join the flow of life and become companions to those who are trying to do the same.

Warrior Boxes

The **Bully** and the **Victim** are strategies for going on from *intimidation* or attacks on our identity. By the Bully I mean the tyrant who mows down all opposition (rather than deceiving or tormenting its prey as the Predator does). By the Victim I mean its opposite, the one who is victimized, weakly refusing to stand its ground. Stewart's box was an example of the Victim. Each is a strategy for proving we're somebody, the Bully by seizing territory, the Victim through a willingness to be a martyr. Films about the Mafia and the military often show us this loop, with both bullies and victims refusing to take full responsibility for their actions. School shootings like the Columbine and Virginia Tech massacres may also show us this loop, as young men who have been repeatedly bullied get fed up, flip into the opposite strategy and mow down their former oppressors.

The **Hothead** and the **Pushover** are strategies for going on from *violations of personal boundaries*. By the Hothead I mean an extreme sensitivity to insult that's spoiling for a fight. By the Pushover I mean its opposite, a willingness to be pushed around without imposing any consequences. Each is a strategy for protecting ourselves, the Hothead by picking fights, the Pushover by sacrificing self-respect and avoiding confrontation. Martial arts films like *Crouching Tiger, Hidden Dragon* sometimes tease at this loop, showing a hero or heroine controlling an impulse to fight against a hotheaded adversary as the audience wonders what it will take to start the fight and if a heated response will render him/her no longer heroic.

All Warrior boxes tell us how strong we are as we serve those around us by letting them shape our identity. In transforming a Warrior box, we learn what is most real, namely, the truth of our inner selves. With this learning, we become able to take full responsibility for our lives and act with integrity toward others.

FOR MORE INFORMATION

For more information on the sixteen boxes, please contact me. Up-to-date contact information is available at www.AlyceBarry.com.

The four archetypes and sixteen boxes are the subject of my forthcoming companion book containing many more examples and exercises, plus personal stories from my Shadow Work colleagues. Please visit www.PracticallyShameless.com for details.

If you have questions about Shadow Work, please contact me or visit the Shadow Work website, www.ShadowWork.com.

Notes

The purpose of these notes is to explain a few essentials without disrupting the main narrative.

With the exception of my family members and friends, the names, personal characteristics and issues of workshop participants have been altered to protect confidentiality.

I have simplified my own story as well as my father's, and this book is not offered as a biography of John Barry. So many factors influence who we become that their inclusion would be quickly overwhelming. My father's parents, his birth order and siblings, his education, religion and ethnic heritage, his marriage and profession, among many other factors, played significant roles in shaping the man he became.

Nearly all of this story is true. The group conversation following my predator process is fictional, as is my thought process sitting by the lake during the first workshop. I don't remember when I came to various realizations and have supplied them as needed to suit the narrative.

CHAPTER 3

I describe Bonnie as being held in a special way by two people so she will not be injured while expressing her anger. I'm referring to the safety hold originally developed by facilitators of the New Warrior Training Adventure (NWTA), the initiation weekend for men run by the ManKind Project (MKP). For more information, visit www.MKP.org.

Experiential processes such as those described throughout this book are often called "carpet work," a term that refers to the common practice of holding a workshop in a carpeted room. Not only does the carpet provide cushioning for a participant or role-players who are seated or kneeling on the floor, but it circumscribes the territory the process will occupy. If it's rectangular, the carpet also symbolically represents the four portals or archetypes.

Another common term for Shadow Work processes is "center-work," which derives from a participant working with facilitators in the center of a group.

Nearly every Shadow Work process begins with what we call a "split," in which a part of the self is seen outside the self played by another person or an object in the room, as for example when Bonnie saw her demon played by Wally. The split is a technique borrowed from gestalt psychotherapy.

Very little has been said in this book about container-building, the careful process of creating a safe emotional environment in which Shadow Work can proceed. At the beginning of a weekend workshop, the facilitators build the container using a variety of group activities over a period of four to six hours before any centerwork is done. In an individual session, a Shadow Work coach builds a safe container by using verbal techniques called "shame-lifters" and talking in depth with the client's Risk Manager.

Whether in a group or individual session, Shadow Work happens in what we call "ritual space," meaning a time and place away from one's daily life during which one can experience parts of the self that have been trapped in boxes without the fear of real-life consequences. The word "ritual" has sometimes carried the negative connotation of a secret ceremony in which participants perform unethical, even illegal acts. The real meaning of "ritual" is an act on the physical plane used to symbolize something that is not of a physical nature. A common example is a birthday cake with lit candles on top, which our culture uses to celebrate a year lived. Imagine explaining to a person from a very different culture why we celebrate a year lived by inserting wax cylinders in a baked confection and setting them on fire!

CHAPTER 8

I have muted the comments of the facilitators in this and other chapters in order to avoid disrupting the narrative, but it might leave the incorrect impression that I was leading myself through the steps of a process without facilitation. Every Shadow Work workshop is led by at least two very highly trained facilitators, and if the group contains both men and women, then the facilitators include at least one man and one woman.

The empowerment process described in Chapter 8 is called a Warrior Run and was developed originally for the NWTA.

CHAPTER 9

This chapter briefly describes my Woman Within Initiation weekend. For more information, visit www.WomanWithin.org. Later in the chapter I undergo a blessing process called Ideal Support, one of half a dozen Sovereign processes used in Shadow Work to help a person let in unconditional support.

CHAPTERS 10 AND 11

These chapters describe what we call a predator or vampire process. When predator energy breaks into compassion, Shadow Work employs a technique we call "the ladder of wants" adapted from Connirae Andreas's book *Core Transformations*.

CHAPTER 13

It is my belief that when Dad ridiculed me, he was feeling irritated by watching me create when he had so little time for his own creative hobbies like woodworking. He might even have chosen carpentry as a profession if he had not had a wife and five children to support. In the twelve-step tradition, they say, "If you spot it, you got it," meaning that we are often more able to see in another person the qualities or behaviors we are not yet ready to see in ourselves. Seeing our issues in others is called projection, and we all engage in it. For years, I felt a great deal of shame whenever I realized I had been projecting. I have come to see that the less shame I feel about my inevitable projections, the more readily I can use my projections to diagnose what is going on with me.

CHAPTER 15

The memorial process described is called the Tombstone process. We know our loved ones in our cells, and our bodies know things about them that our minds do not. The Tombstone process is available on a CD from the Shadow Work online store. One example of a ritual component in a Shadow Work process is the use of a piece of fabric in the Tombstone process to symbolize a box we are giving back to a loved one.

As is no doubt evident from the processes described in this book, Shadow Work is experiential, meaning the workshop participant or client learns through experiencing while having the guidance and support of a skilled facilitator. Moving physically through a process, by stepping into a part or moving to another part of the room, gives it a power it would not otherwise have.

CHAPTER 19

For music during the exercise, my favorites are "Gabriel's Oboe" by Ennio Morricone from the soundtrack to *The Mission*; "Part One" by Constance Demby from *Novus Magnificat: Through the Stargate*; "O Magnum Mysterium" by Morten Lauridsen from *Lux Aeterna*; the Adagio movement of Beethoven's Ninth Symphony; and the Largo movement of Dvorak's Ninth ("New World") Symphony.

Acknowledgments

My gratitude to Cliff Barry extends to far more than creating the model that is the subject of this book and writing an inspired Foreword. Cliff has been there for me in almost every way imaginable: first as my older brother; later as my trainer and mentor; as a key player in my support system through several tough transitions; and finally as my friend, colleague, champion and financial backer. For all this there aren't enough ways to say thank you.

Special thanks go also to my daughter, Joanna Swift, for her unwavering confidence in me, and to my brother, Tim Barry, a skillful and compassionate listener who helped me stay in one piece as I finished and then laid this beloved burden down. My brilliant friend and colleague Susan DeGenring has been a crucial source of perspective and encouragement. Thanks also to my wonderful editor, David Hicks, who has the extraordinary gift of encouraging a new author while gently pointing the manuscript toward a workable book, and to my friend Melanie Mulhall for fixing so brilliantly my peculiarities of phrasing, grammar and punctuation in a final edit. Thanks also to my talented and companionable design team, Nick Zelinger and Cindy Kalman, who have been a delight to work with.

Jude Blitz and Marie-Françoise Rosat are foremost among the colleagues who listened and cheered me on through this long process. Financial support has come from Vicki Woodard and others, listed on the Supporters page at www.PracticallyShameless.com. Joe Laur, Martin Lassoff, Ginny Drewes, Sharanjit Paddam, Jeff Baugher,

Valerie Young, Becky Schupbach, Janine Romaner, Jeff Manchester, Steve Kushner, Marilyn Paul, Dave and Chrissy McFarren, and John and Nicola Kurk were among the other colleagues who have given me useful insights and support.

Thank you also to George Rounds and Pauline LeBlanc for giving me the opportunity to talk about Shadow Work at the International Coach Federation and Hands On Therapy, where I first began to put these ideas into story form and grasp that I could reach a general audience.

Finally, thanks to so many others who encouraged and supported me during this long process, particularly Gail Duffy-Solak, Bill Kauth, Lyman Coleman, Jo Mortland, Krystala Kalil, Sally Anne Thompson, Susan Snyder, Mark Robers, Megara Kastner, Mary Walilko, Margaret Adams, Steve and Debra Truax, Gloria Barry, Amina Knowlan, Arlyn Heideman, Scott Weaver, Rhonda Hess, Seth Henry, Michele Nahas, and Aubrey Swift. I've received enormously helpful input on writing and publishing, most recently from Kabir Jaffe, Rosemary Carstens, Barbara Wilder and Barbara Darling, and over the years from Chuck Ebert, Joe Marshall, Charles Dyke, Oliver Franklin and most especially from Douglas Messerli.

Index

About the Author

A lyce Barry is a writer, speaker and Shadow Work facilitator in Longmont, Colorado, giving workshops and individual sessions. As a speaker, Alyce has delighted general and professional audiences with her engaging personal style and her compelling insights about the shadow illustrated with easy-to-understand images and examples. As one person has said, "Alyce puts flesh on Jung's bones." Contact Alyce about speaking to your group, organization or conference at www.AlyceBarry.com/Contact.

Look for the companion workbook to *Practically Shameless* and other titles from Practically Shameless Press. Alyce's blogs can be found at www.AlyceBarry.com and www.PracticallyShameless.com.

PRACTICALLY SHAMELESS

PRESS

Quick Order Form

Phone orders: Call (303) 485-5400
Web orders: www.PracticallyShameless.com
Mail orders: Practically Shameless Press
PO Box 1505
Longmont CO 80502-1505, USA

Name:_____

Address:_____

_____

City:_____ State/Province_____

Zip/Postal Code_____Country_____

Telephone:_____

Email address:_____

____ copies of *Practically Shameless: How Shadow Work Helped Me Find My Voice, My Path, and My Inner Gold* – **$16.95** per copy   _____

Colorado residents, add sales tax of **$1.36** per copy   _____

Shipping to U.S./Canadian addresses:
    $3.00 for the first copy   _____
    $2.00 for each additional copy   _____
Shipping to addresses outside the U.S./Canada:
    $11.00 for the first copy   _____
    $6.00 for each additional copy   _____

                                                    TOTAL   _____

____ Check enclosed
____ Please bill my credit card:
    Card number_____
    Expiration date_____ /_____
    Signature_____

Please also send me FREE information on:
____ Speaking engagements
____ Shadow Work sessions with Alyce Barry
____ Shadow Work workshops and classes with Alyce Barry
____ Shadow Work facilitation trainings